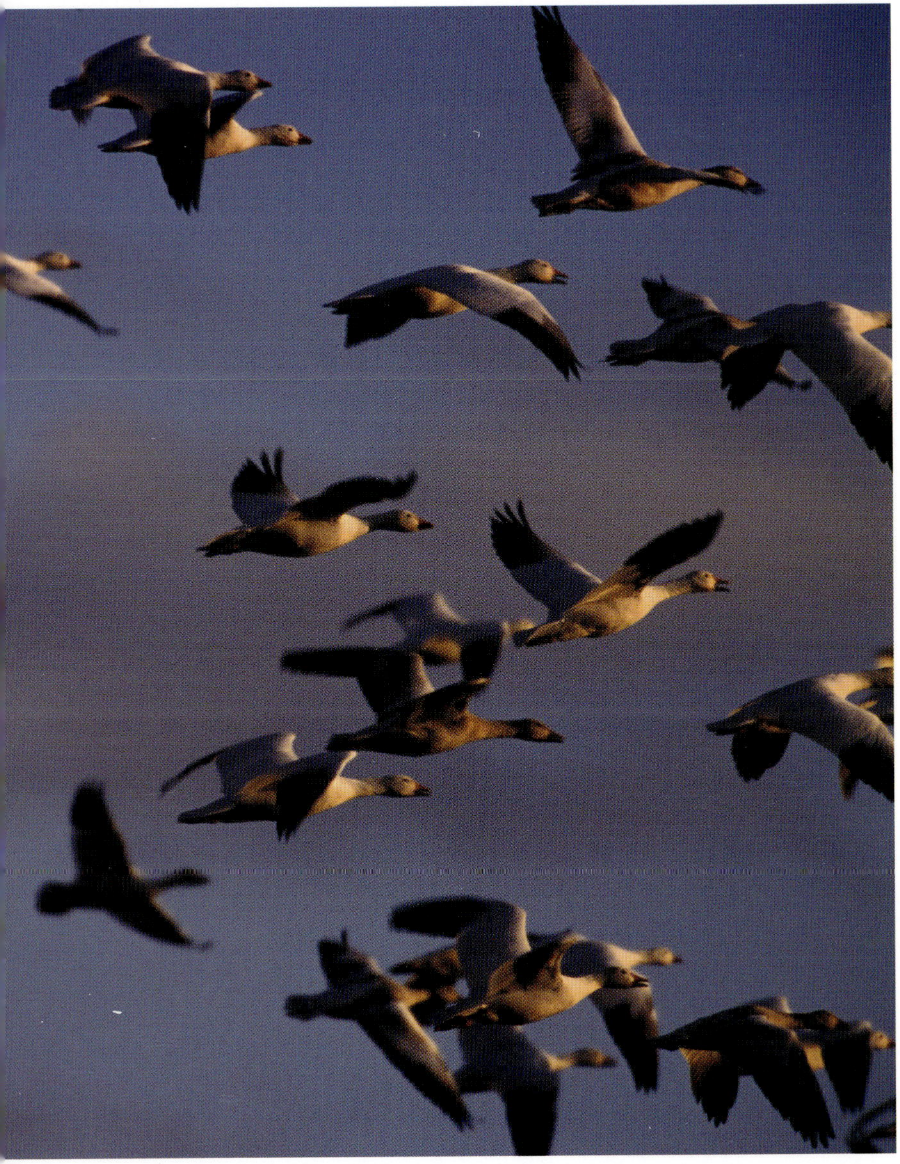

Bosque del Apache

National Wildlife Refuge

48 Hours of Flight

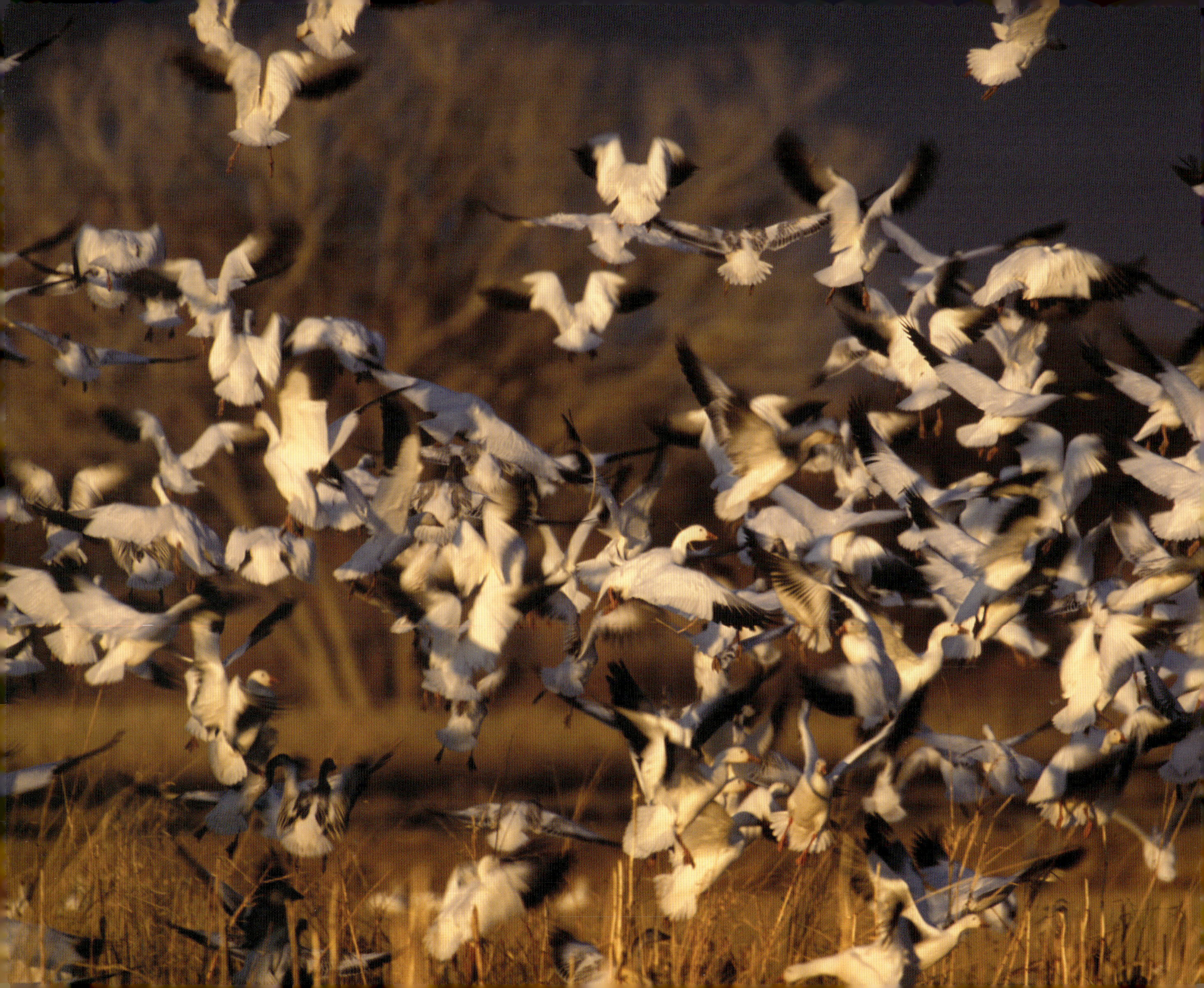

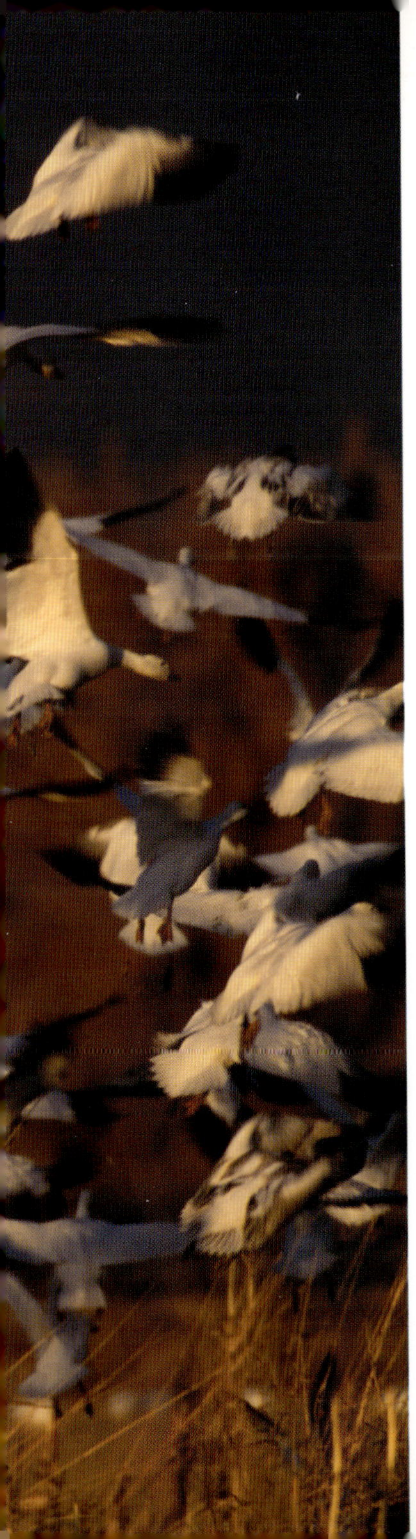

Bosque del Apache
National Wildlife Refuge
48 Hours of Flight

JIM JAMIESON

IMAGESTREAM PRESS
SAVAGE, MINNESOTA

Typeset in Adobe Garamond

First published in 2003 by ImageStream Press
8339 Carriage Hill Alcove
Savage, MN 55378
jjamieson@compuserve.com

For extra copies of this book please check with your preferred bookstore, or write ImageStream Press.

Printed in China
by C & C Offset Printing Co., LTD.

Illustrations
Cover: Sandhill Cranes at Daybreak, Bosque del Apache National Wildlife Refuge
Page 1: Snow Geese in Flight
Page 2-3: Snow Geese Spooked in the Late Afternoon

This book is dedicated to my wife Julie, and sons Ian and Wesley whose endless patience and understanding helped to make this work become a reality. Special thanks to the staff of Bosque del Apache National Wildlife Refuge.

All wildlife photographs herein were done so under free ranging, non-captive situations.

In celebration of the 100th anniversary of the U.S. Fish and Wildlife Service National Wildlife Refuge System.

Publisher's Cataloging-in-Publication
(Provided by Quality Books, Inc.)

Jamieson, Jim
Bosque del Apache National Wildlife Refuge : 48 hours of flight / Jim Jamieson.
p. cm.
LCCN 2003102775
ISBN 0-9729126-0-6

1. Birds--New Mexico--Bosque del Apache National Wildlife Refuge--Pictorial works. 2. Bosque del Apache National Wildlife Refuge (N.M.)--Pictorial works.
I. Title

QL684.N6J36 2003 598'.09789'62
QBI33-1256

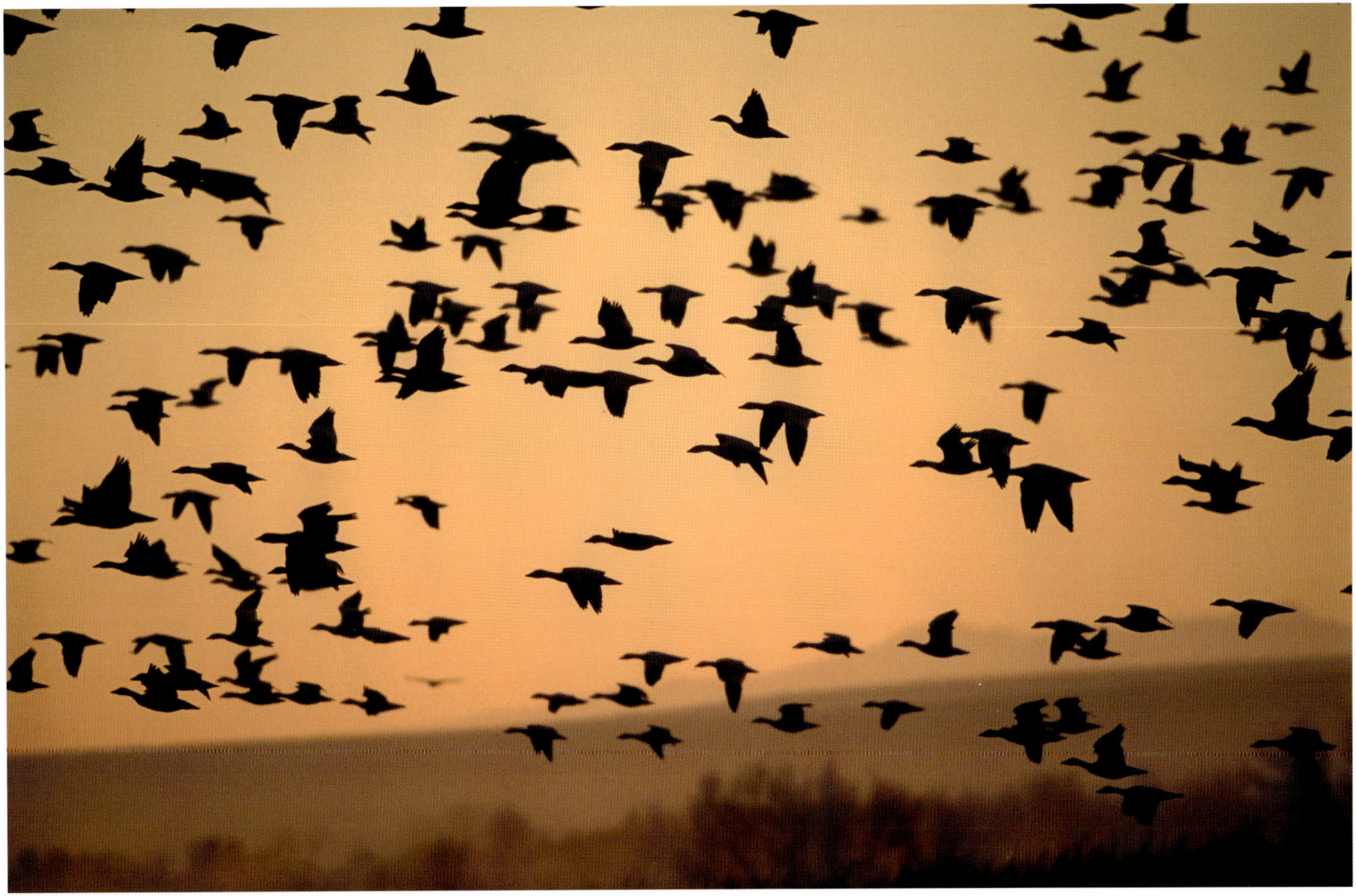

Above: Thousands of Snow Geese streak across the New Mexico sky on a cold, clear December morning.

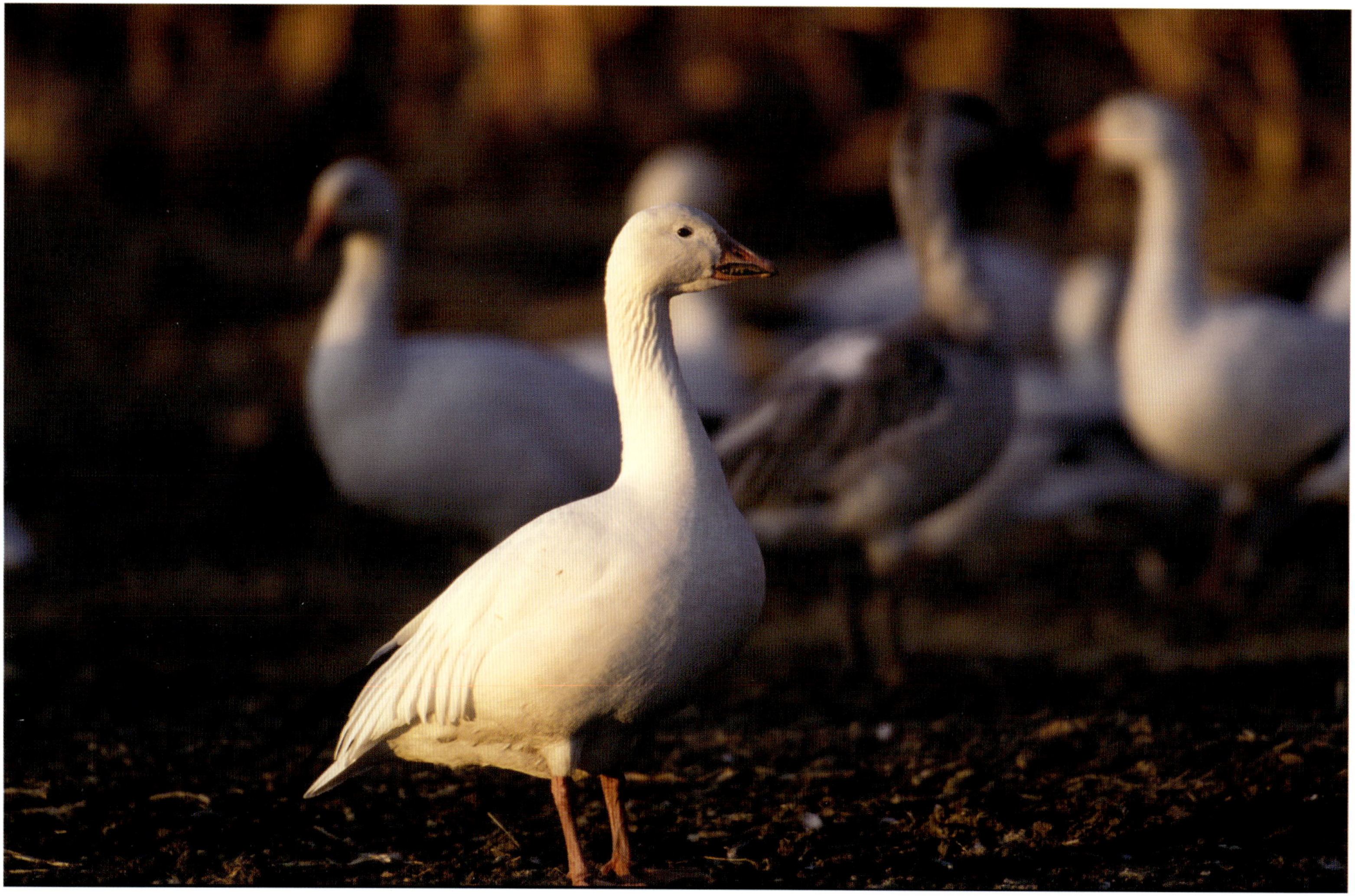

Above: In the late afternoon sun, Snow and Ross' Geese populate the cornfields of Bosque del Apache National Wildlife Refuge. Breeding in the harsh arctic tundra of North America, these birds have migrated thousands of miles to central New Mexico to winter along the Rio Grande.

Contents

Introduction

There are few places across the United States that can match the stunning display of cranes, geese, ducks, and raptors than at Bosque del Apache National Wildlife Refuge in central New Mexico. In the fall, as the days shorten and temperatures drop, Sandhill Cranes and Snow Geese from the central flyway converge on this land adjacent to the Rio Grande river. As if an island in an otherwise desert of barren land, a critical asset of life is provided, water. In early December, the convergence of wildlife overwhelms the refuge. Magnificent thunders of birds, the ancestral honking of cranes, and the sinister flight of hawks and Northern Harriers bring life to the refuge.

In the span of 48 hours of daylight, these photographs document the rhythms of life on the refuge. From sun up to sun down, the patterns of movement and interaction have been captured. From the roar of geese flying out at sunrise, midday herons, raptors, and sunset flights, the refuge is in a constant rhythm of life. Occasionally there were interruptions. Like any eco-system, the survival of life is inter-related across species. As a coyote moves in to attempt a kill on a Snow Goose, or an eagle flies low and fast across the flock, the course of life can be interrupted. Suddenly, thousands of birds take to flight in an unpredictable and often erratic flight path. As if at a football game during kick-off, the roar of birds can be deafening. Launching into the air, the sky darkens in seemingly utter confusion. In the safety of flight, order returns.

Capturing these images in a 48 hour period was a challenge. Rising at 5am against an ink black sky, it was hard to imagine life could be so abundant in these lands. In darkness, I would join other photographers from around the world to capture on film, and the latest in digital cameras, the wonderful display of color and life. Cold soaked, photographic equipment was often prone to failure. Loss of battery power, camera mounts that move slower, film advance mechanisms malfunctioning, and minimal light, all occurring while the cold drives pain and numbness.

With daybreak arriving, frost would slowly melt off the camera lens housings. The sound of birds and shutters signals a new day. At the Flight Deck viewing platform, photographers jockey large 500 and 600mm lenses for position as the sunrise ignites thousands of birds into flight. For those fortunate to return day after day, the vivid colors, action, and rhythms of life can be prone to fading with excitement. In bounding this work to 48 hours, my hope was to capture this excitement on film for a lifetime.

In the morning, large transients of birds would fly out to feed in the fields surrounding the refuge. From vantage points all around the refuge it is possible to see and photograph the magnificent flight of these birds. As late morning and midday approaches, raptors and ducks move to center stage while Snow Geese and cranes populate farmlands. Raptors take up surveillance positions searching out prey along with herons scanning small streams. Suddenly, the sun hangs low in the December sky. As the New Mexican landscape explodes in color, the intensity of life increases one again. Through the cold, clear night skies, a new day arrives.

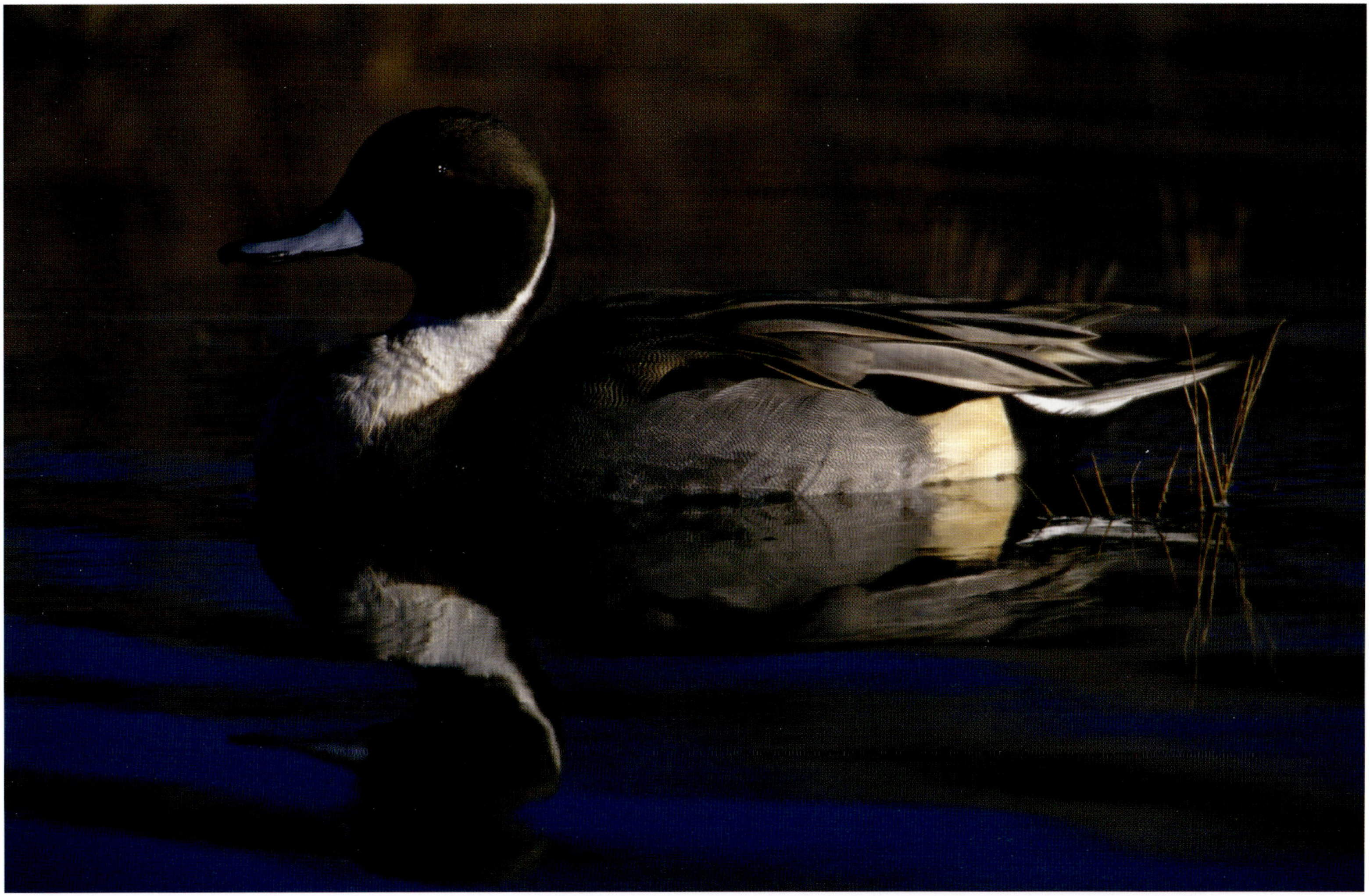

Above: Bosque del Apache is home to a wide array of migrating ducks, geese, and raptors from November through March. Late in the day Northern Pintails frequent numerous ponds and lakes on the refuge. Feeding along the shore, the pintails are rarely disturbed by vehicles on the auto loop tour. Using the vehicle as a bird blind, it is possible to photograph at close range while not creating a disturbance.

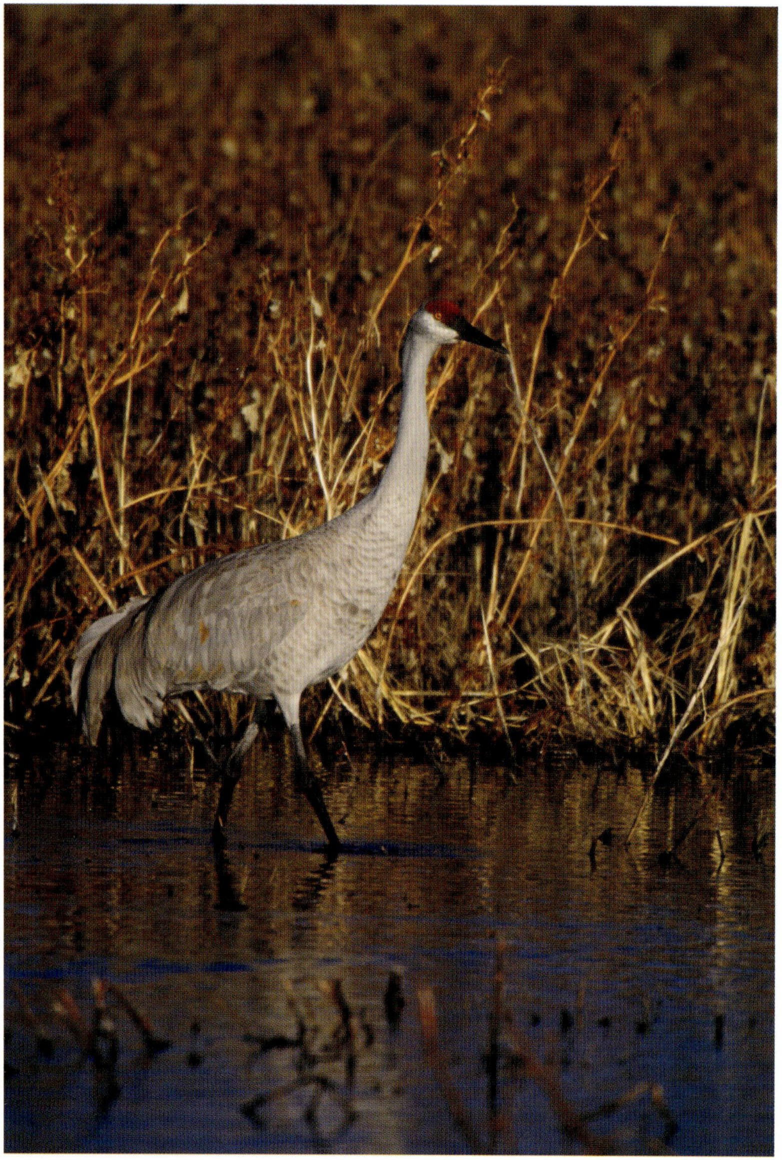

Left: Along the 15 mile auto route, public viewing platforms offer spectacular views of the refuge. Amply named, the Flight Deck platform offers an incredible view of this primary fly-way. In the morning and evening, thousands of cranes and geese launch into an overwhelming array of flight. Nearby, a lone Sandhill Crane wades quietly in the water in preparation for the nightly fly-in.

Right: Bosque del Apache provides a key ingredient for cranes, birds, and other wildlife, water. Surrounded by desert and the meandering Rio Grande, the refuge is an ideal location to winter.

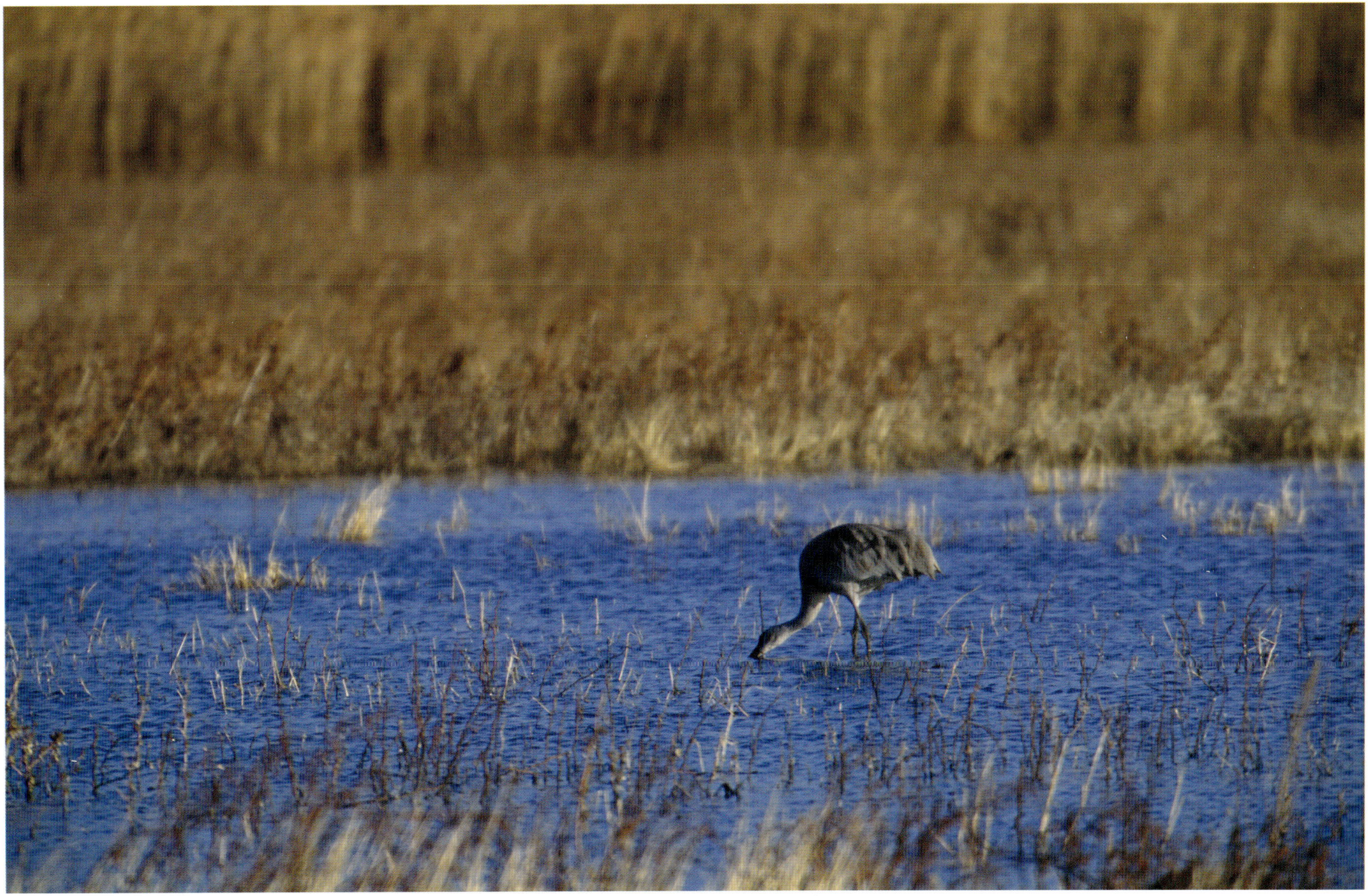

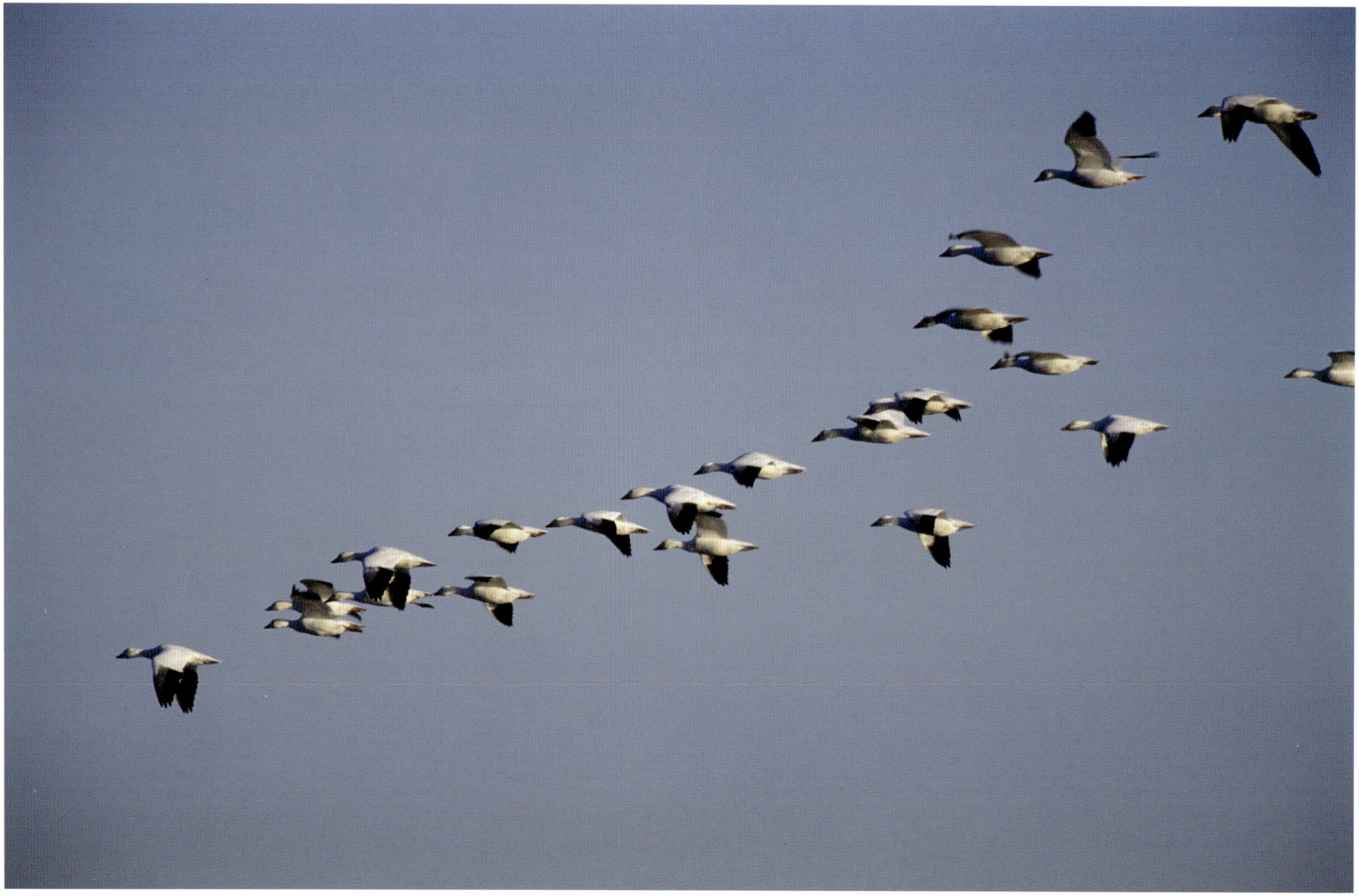

Left: As the sun hangs low on the refuge, the snow geese return from their feeding grounds to the north to spend the night in the protection of water.

Right: Large and small flocks make the journey across the refuge to take up residence several hundred meters down range of the Flight Deck.

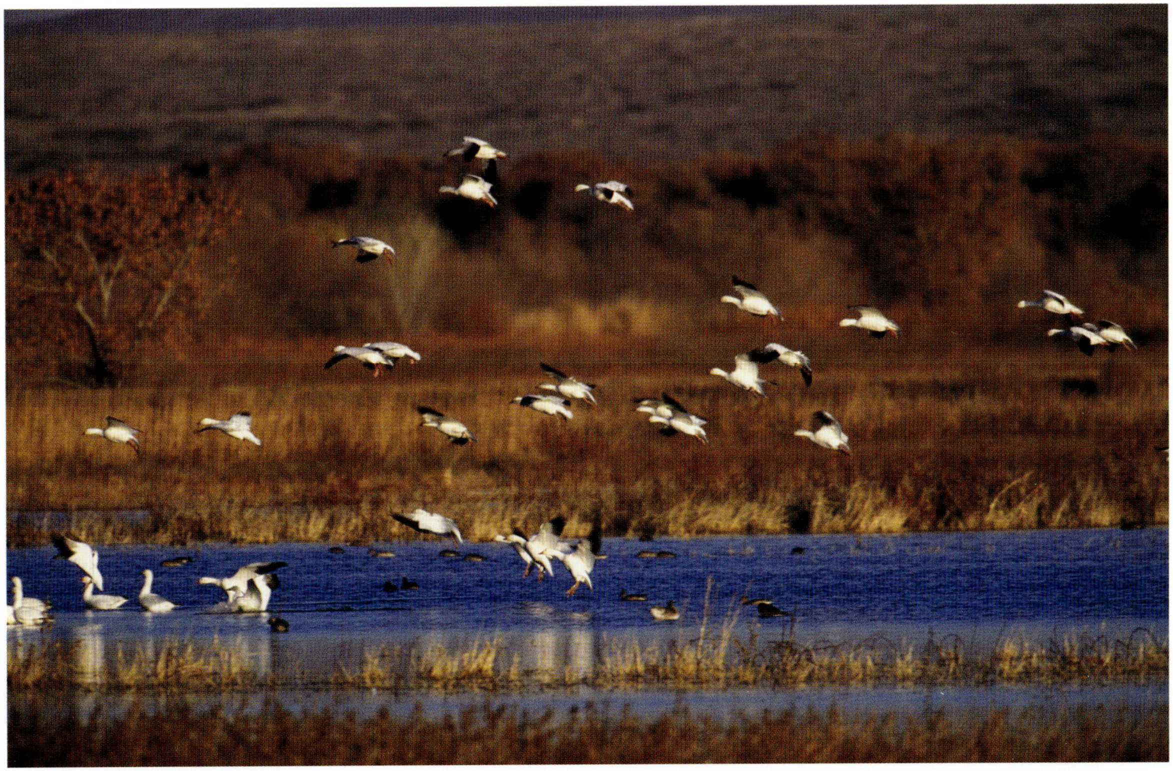

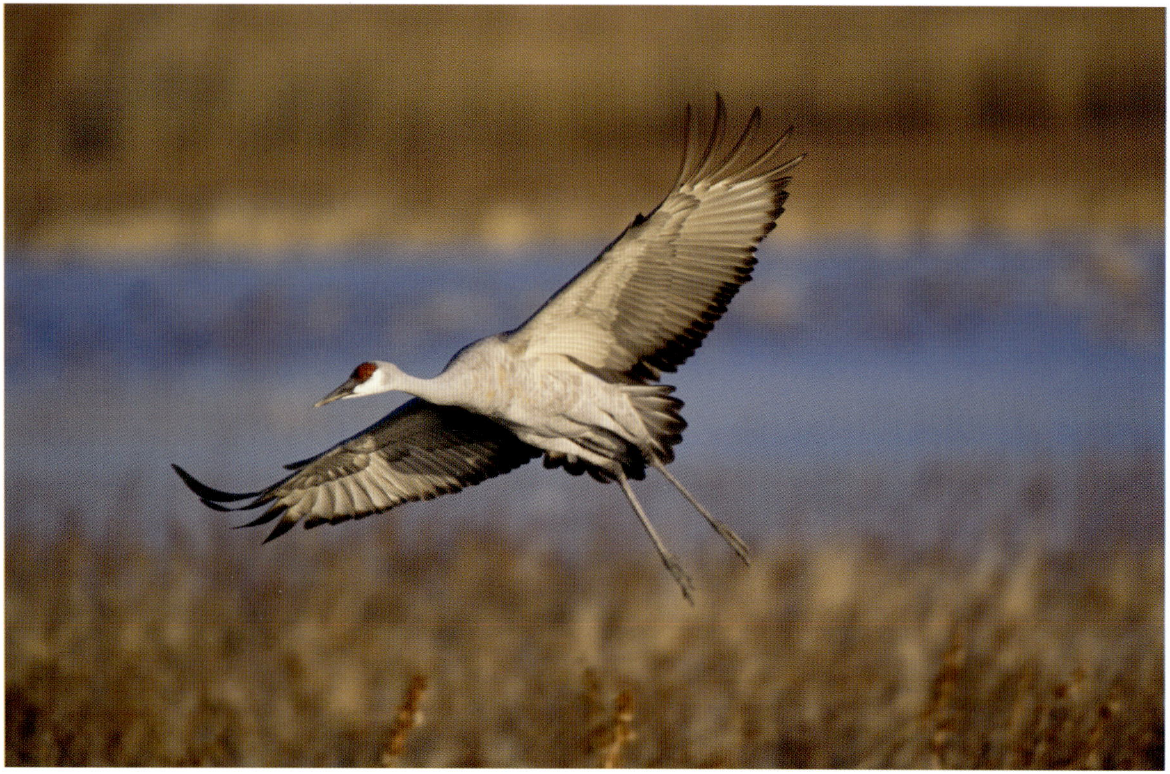

Left: Following close behind the Snow Geese, a Sandhill Crane quietly swoops in to join the other crane in front of the Flight Deck.

Right: Folding the wings, the crane quickly stalls the lift and descends into the marsh water.

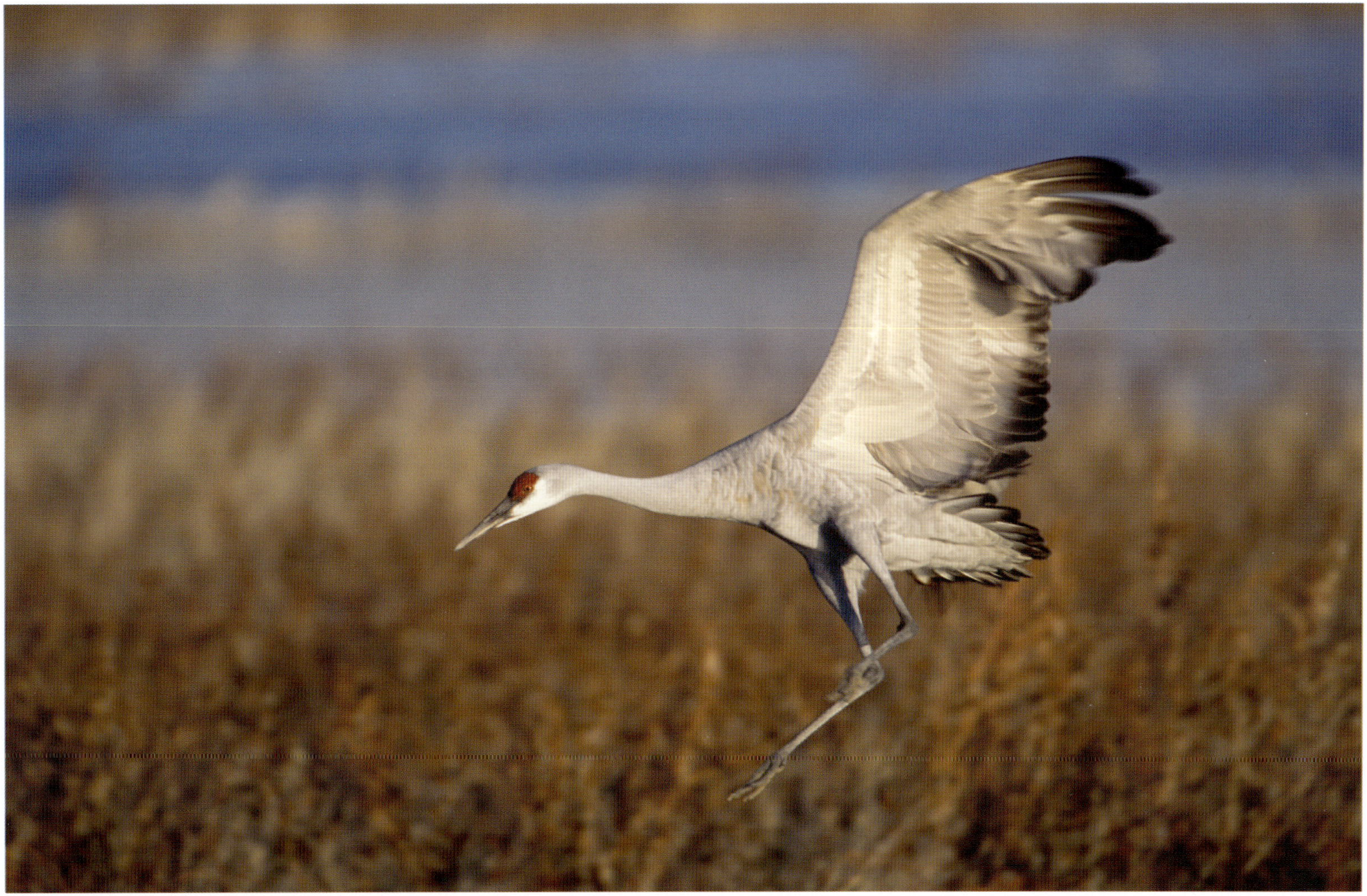

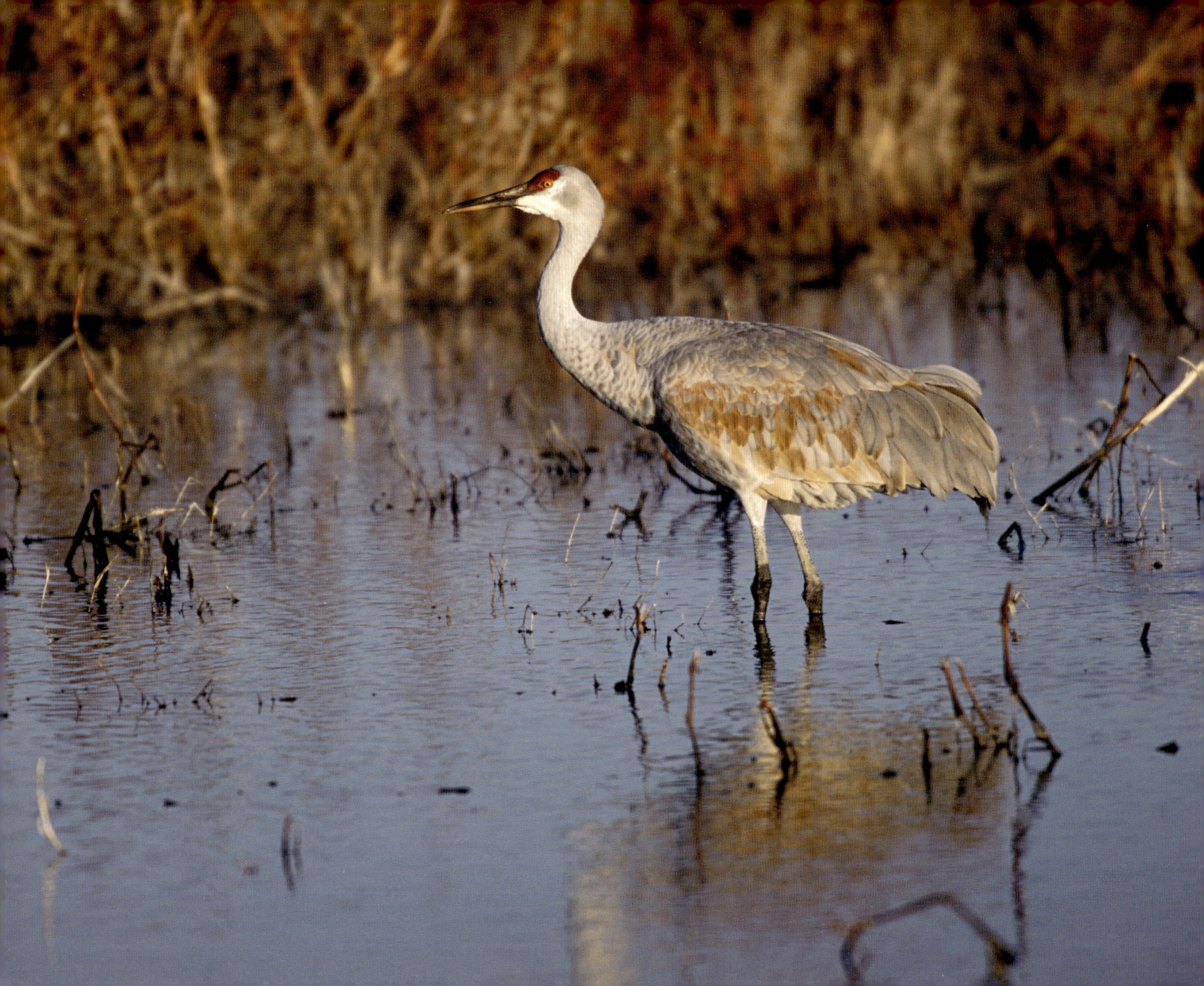

Left: Once on the ground, the cranes move quietly, carefully observing the area while taking on water.

Right: Late in the day, the sun bathes the cranes in golden light. Mating for life, they carry on a very social relationship of courtship dances. With a life span of 20 years, they have an opportunity to return to the refuge for many years to come.

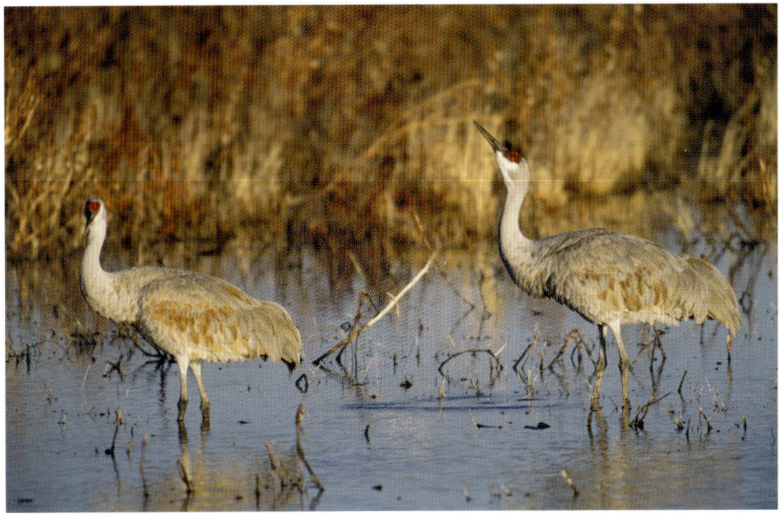

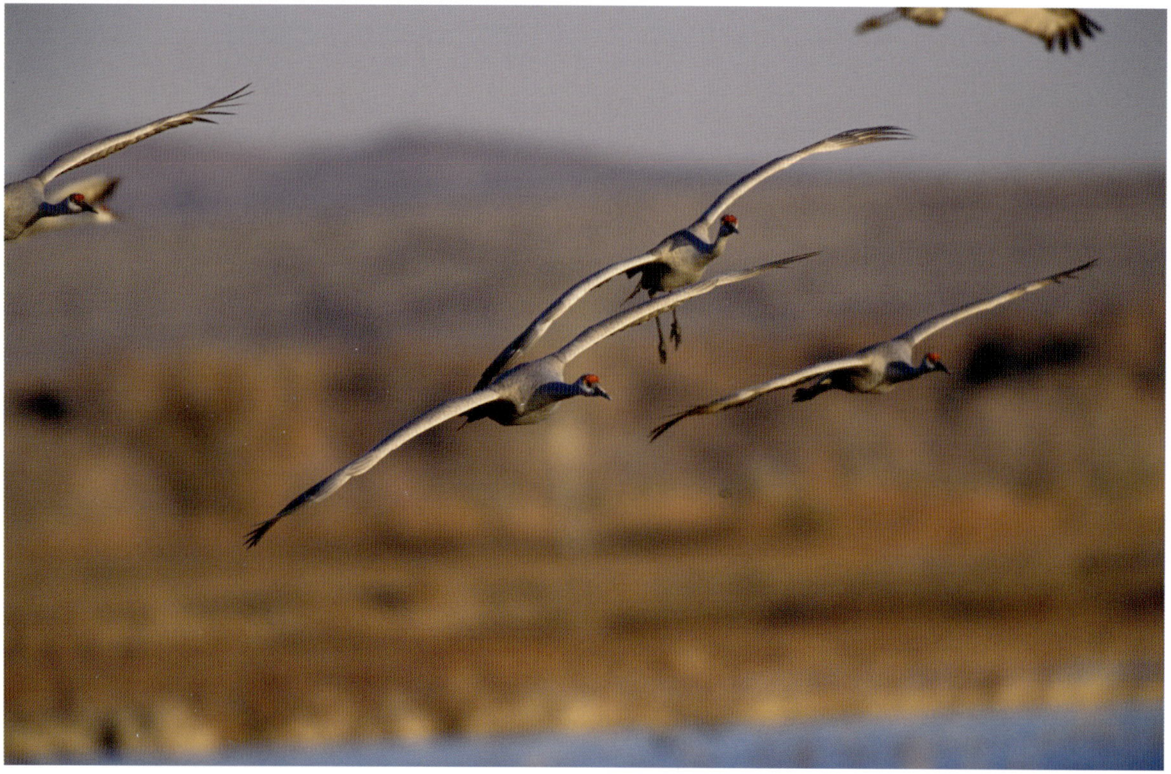

Above: Suddenly, from the left a flock of cranes approaches the area. Calling out, they setup on final approach and quickly descend into the marsh.

Right: As the group of cranes trace along the marsh, they carefully watch the photographers on the viewing platform. Never threatened, they attend to the business at hand of locating a place to roost for the night.

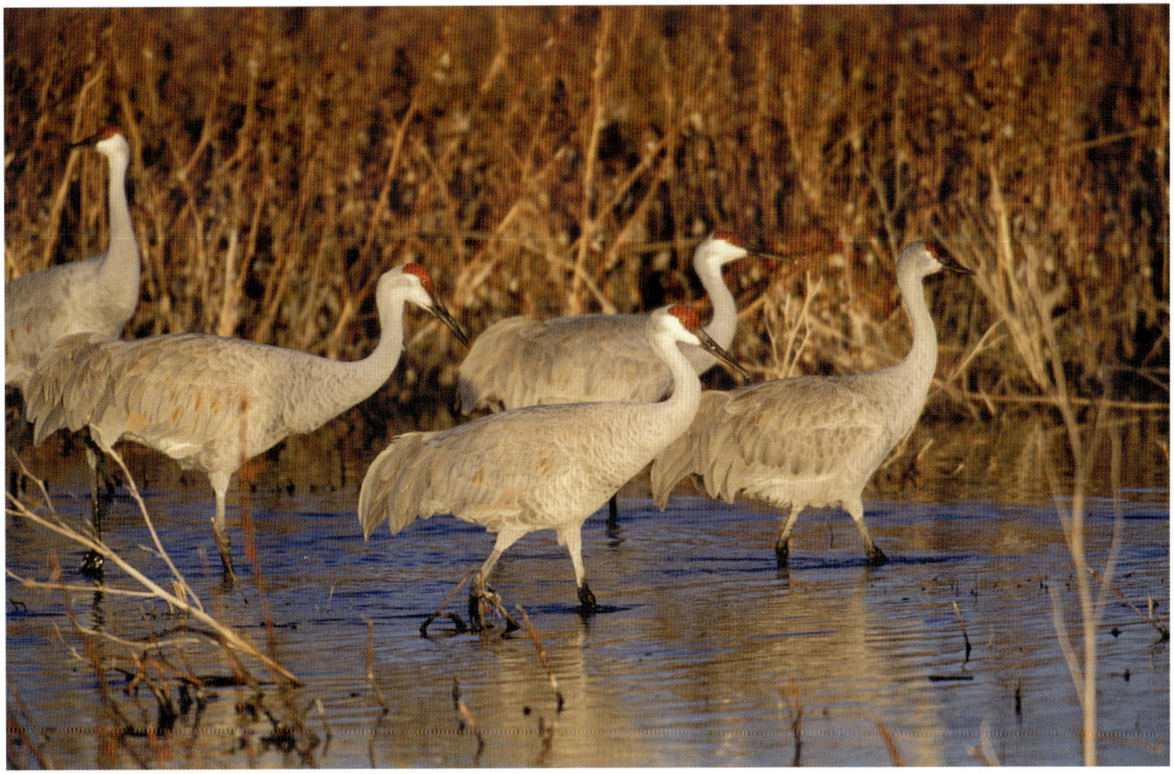

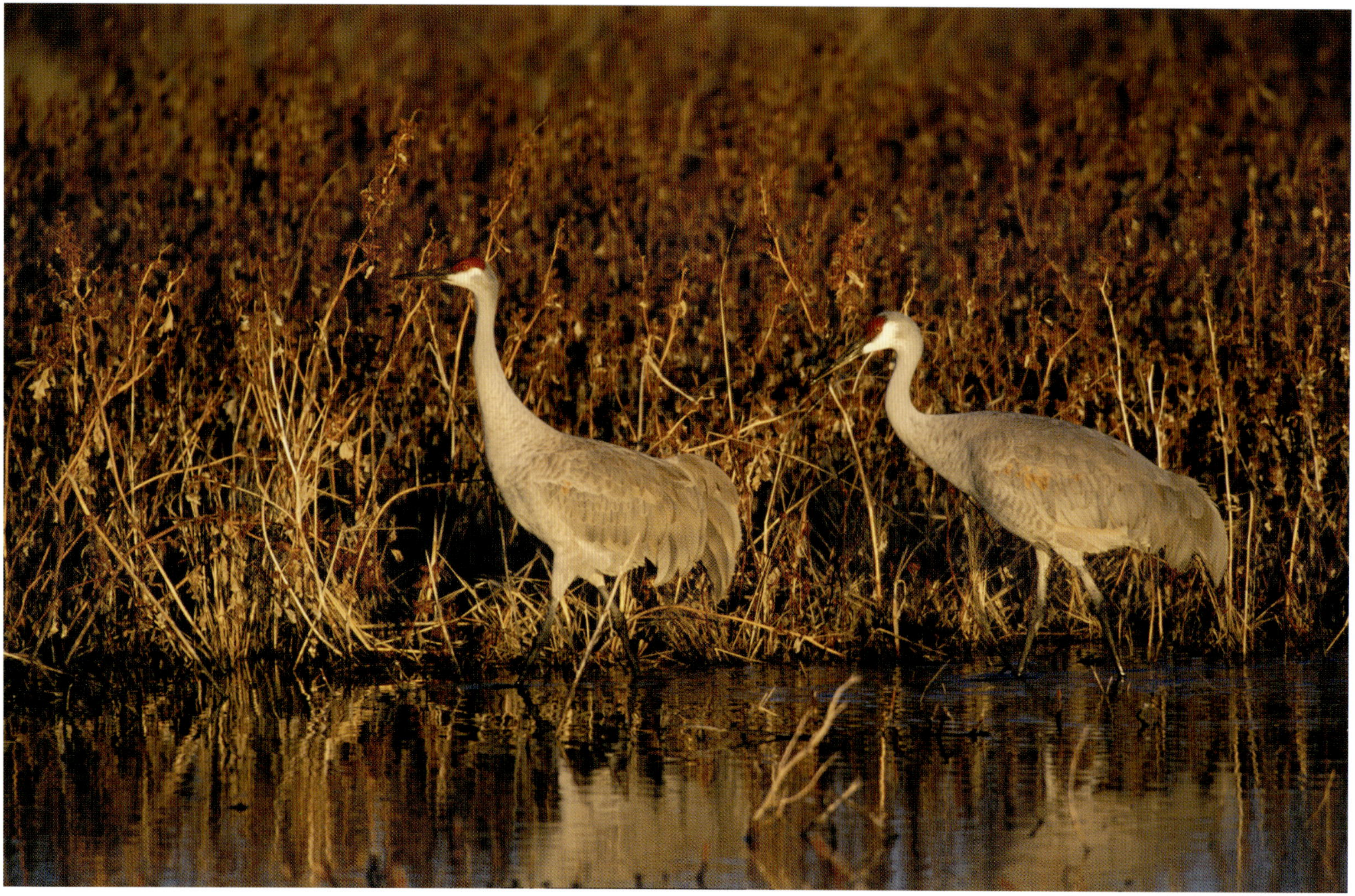

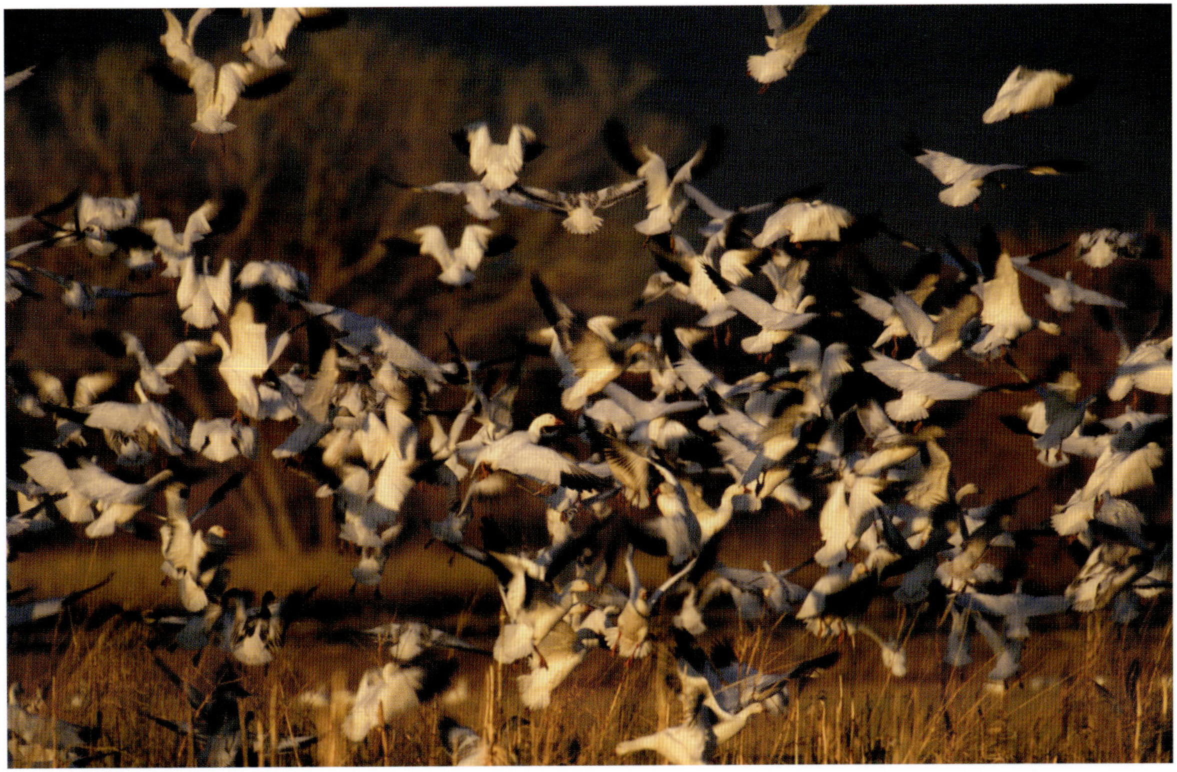

Above: With 13,000 acres to cover on the refuge, Snow and Ross' Geese have settled into the northern farmlands and cornfields. Occasionally smaller flocks take to flight in an uproar. Once airborne, they circle returning to the same area.

Left: Late in the day the sunlight illuminates the cranes in a golden glow. As daylight quickly recedes, film speed and aperture become very important for the photographer. Difficult for film cameras to change mid-roll, ISO speeds quickly approach 800. Soon, fast action flight will turn to a blur.

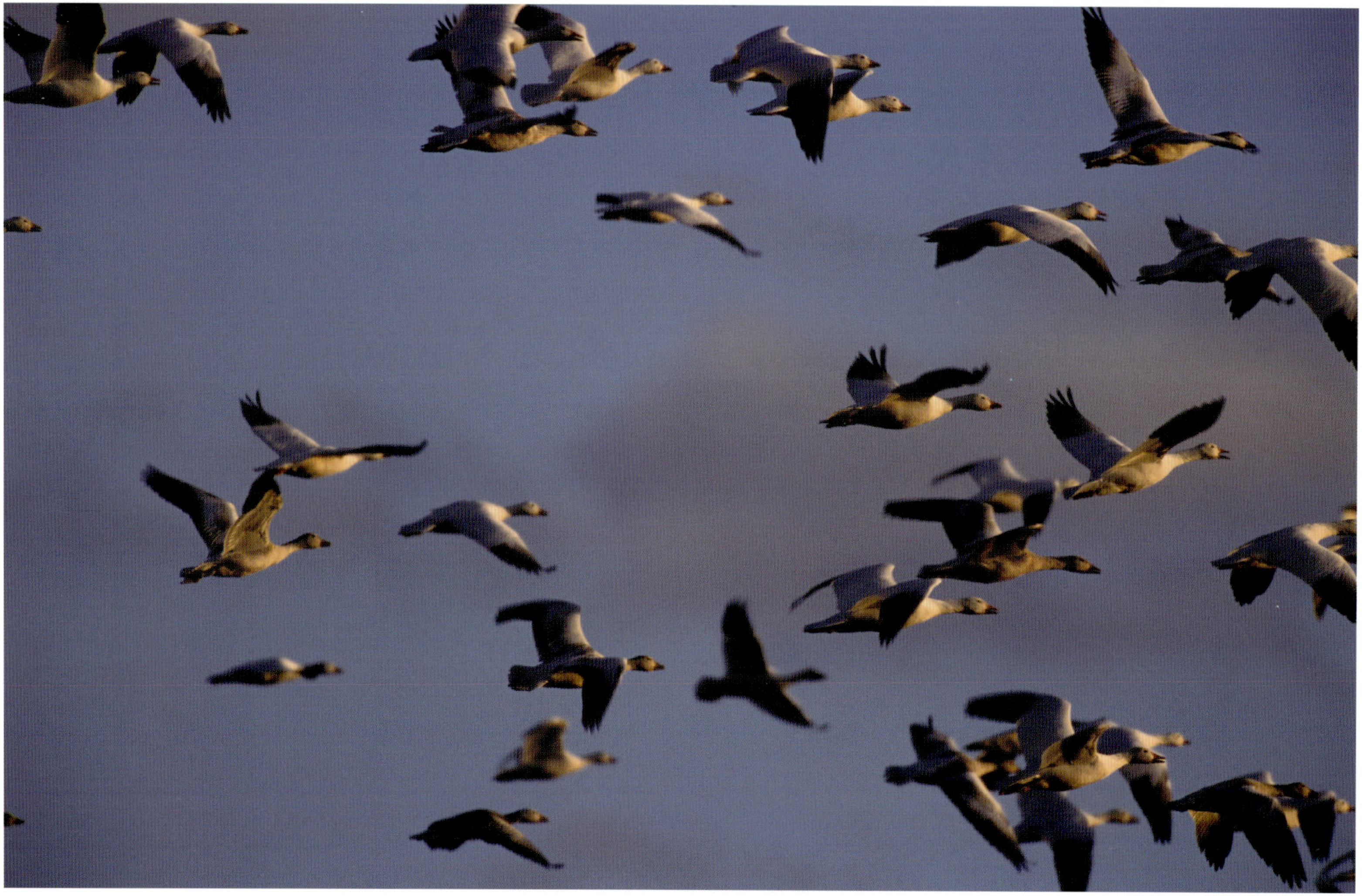

Left: From vantage points all across the refuge, Snow Geese and cranes are airborne for the nightly fly-in against a colorful New Mexico sky. At dawn and dusk, the birds are in constant motion.

Right: Rarely at ease, the Snow Geese get ready to rest for the evening.

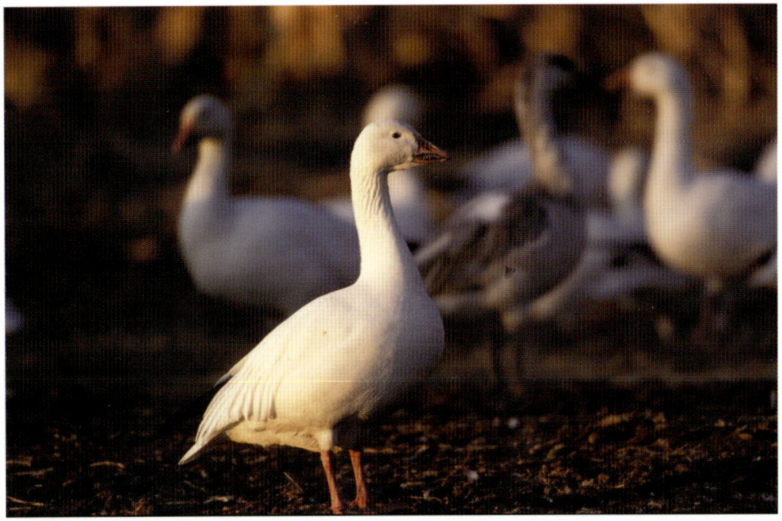

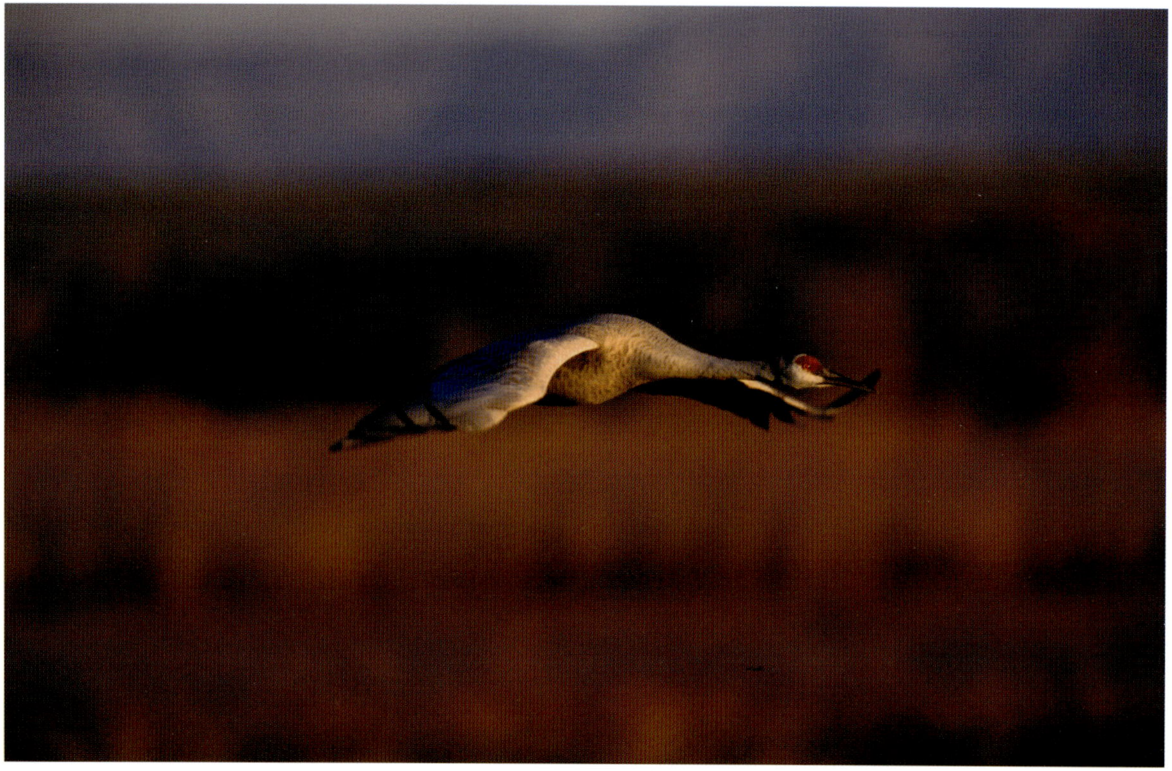

Above: Crane, after crane, with stealth and an occasional call, the birds glide on final approach to the marsh. The Flight Deck is a primary area for visitors and photographers alike to view a continuous stream of cranes coming into roost. From this vantage point, cranes, geese, pintails, Northern Shovelers, and Northern Harriers are in a constant theater of motion.

Right: Late in the day the features on the cranes are replaced with graceful silhouettes. Outstretched to the sky, this crane takes a well needed drink.

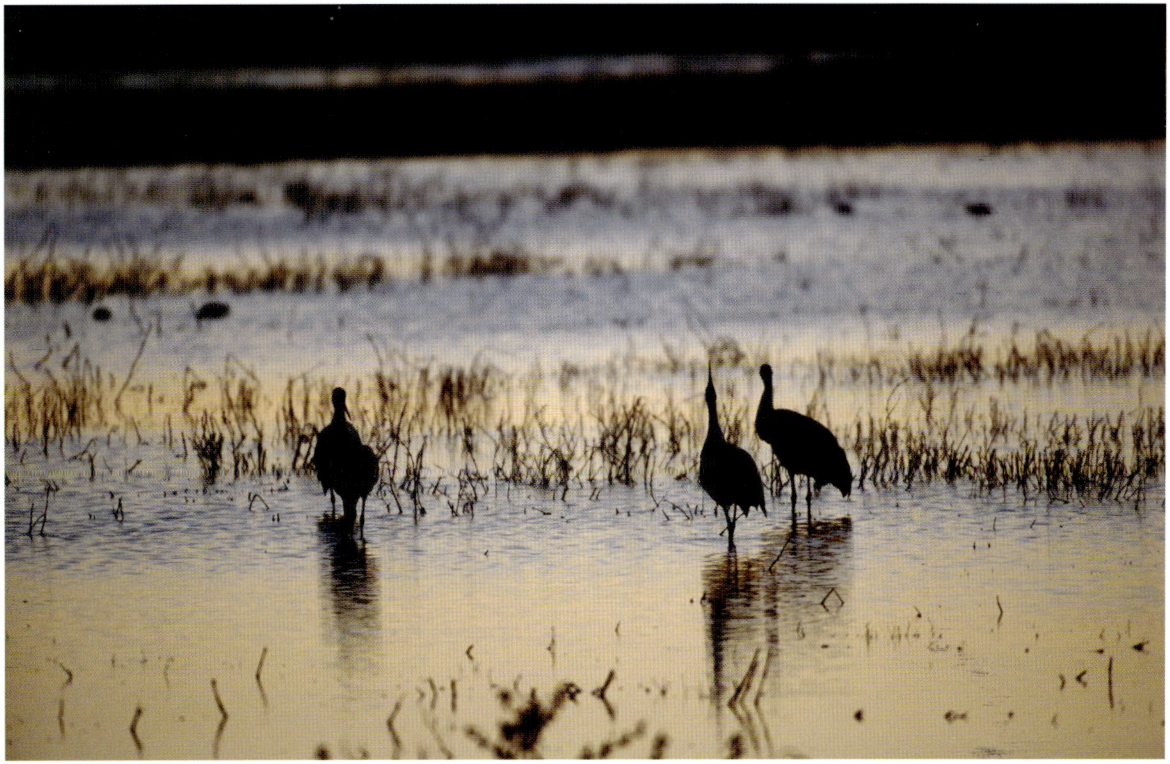

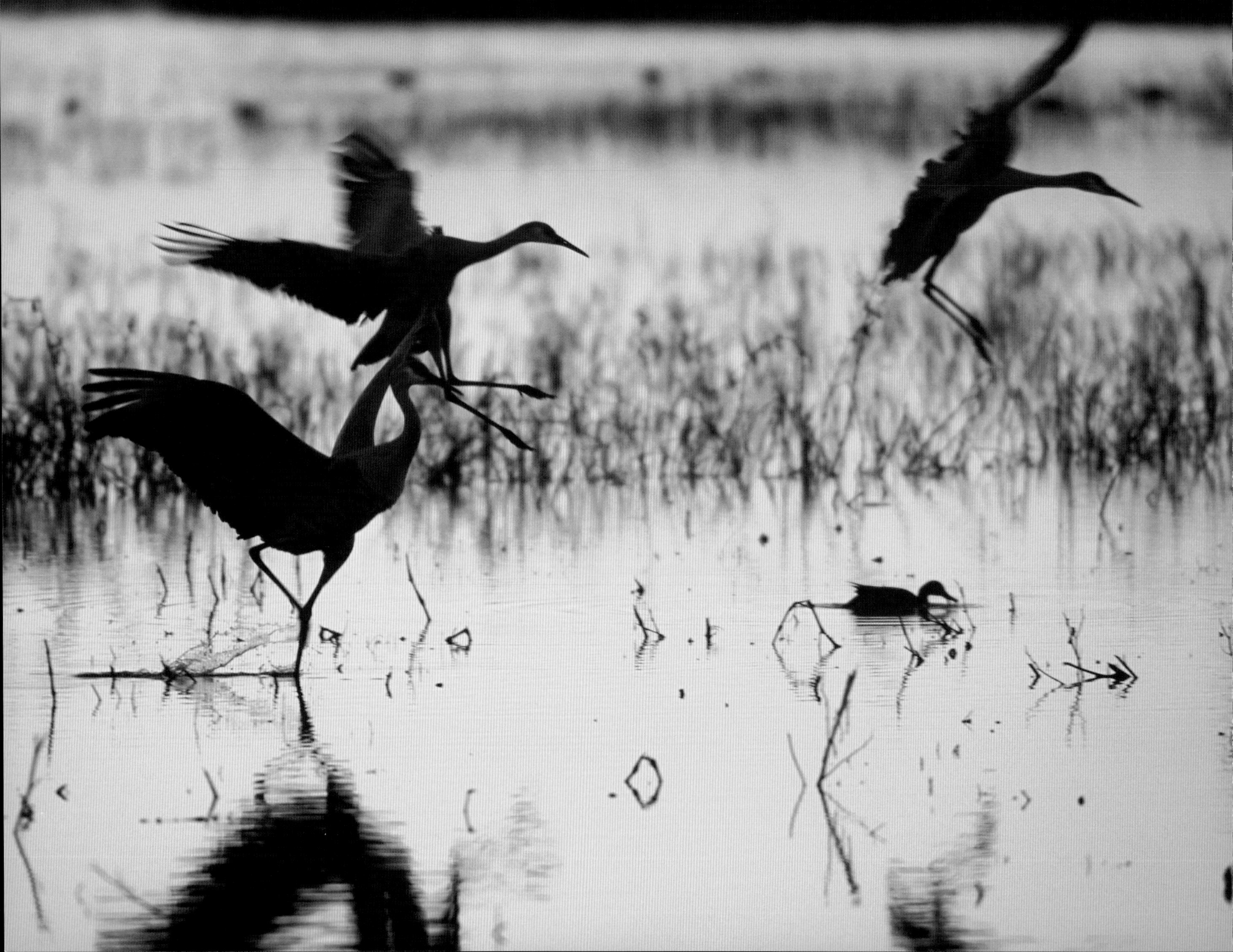

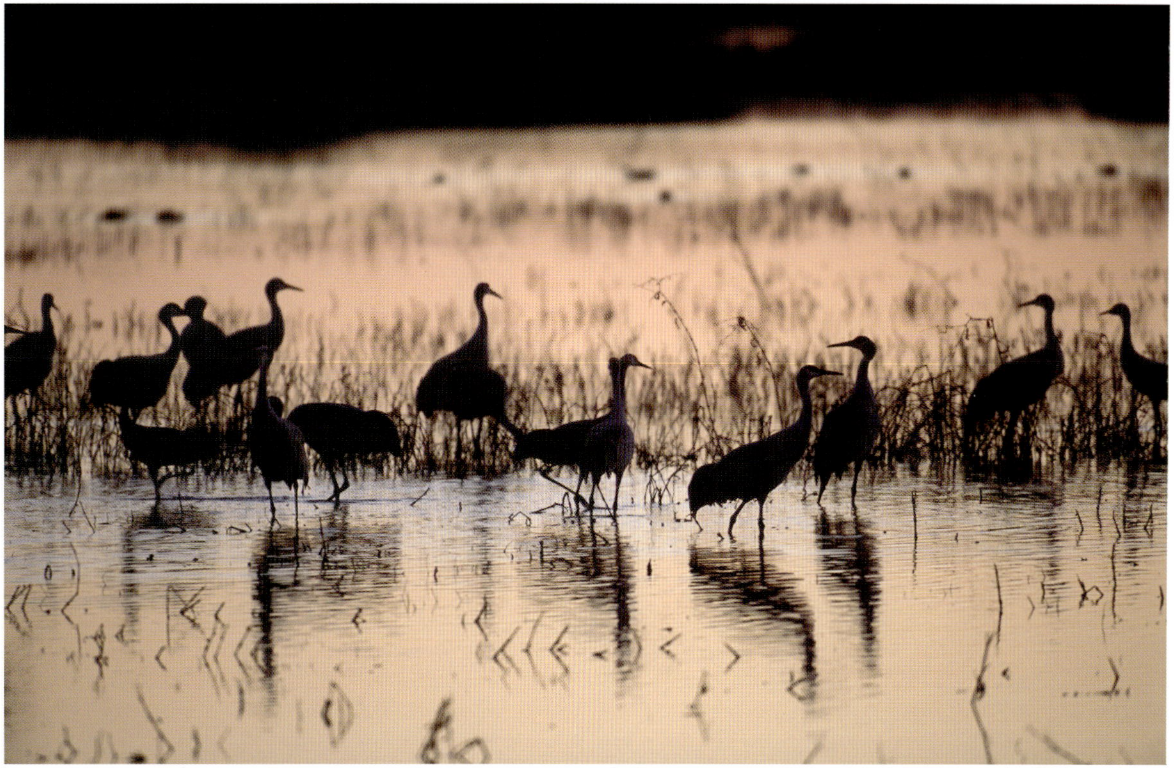

Above: A sizeable flock has formed in preparation for the cold, long night. In constant communication, the cranes signal to one another through verbal and nonverbal methods.

Left: As the birds approach the landing zone, a delicate midair dance occurs to break the speed and join the flock.

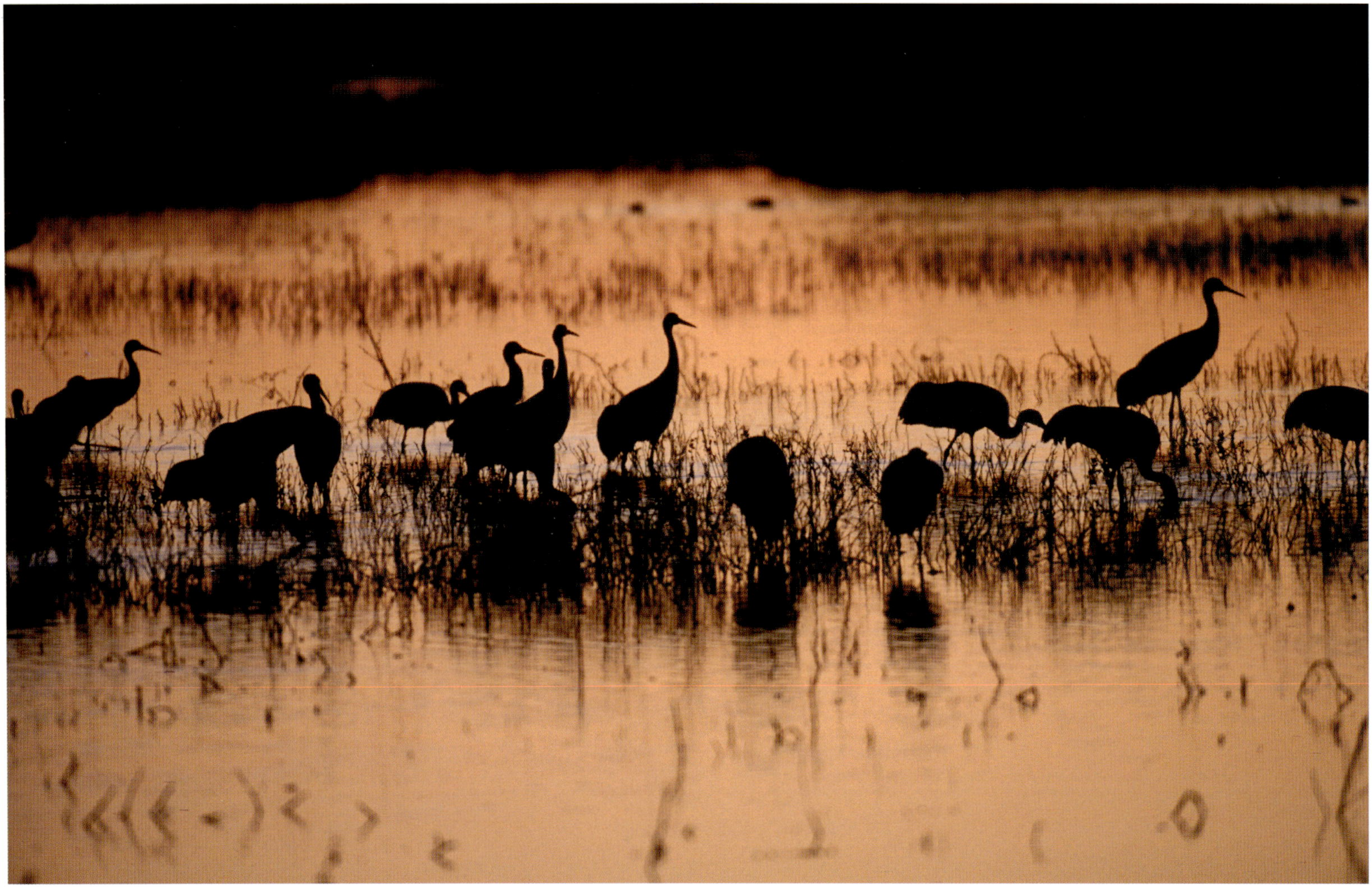

Left: Slowly, the grey and red plumage gives way to black silhouettes moving against an ever deepening red sky.

Below: In a last call of the day, several cranes look to the sky expelling one final message.

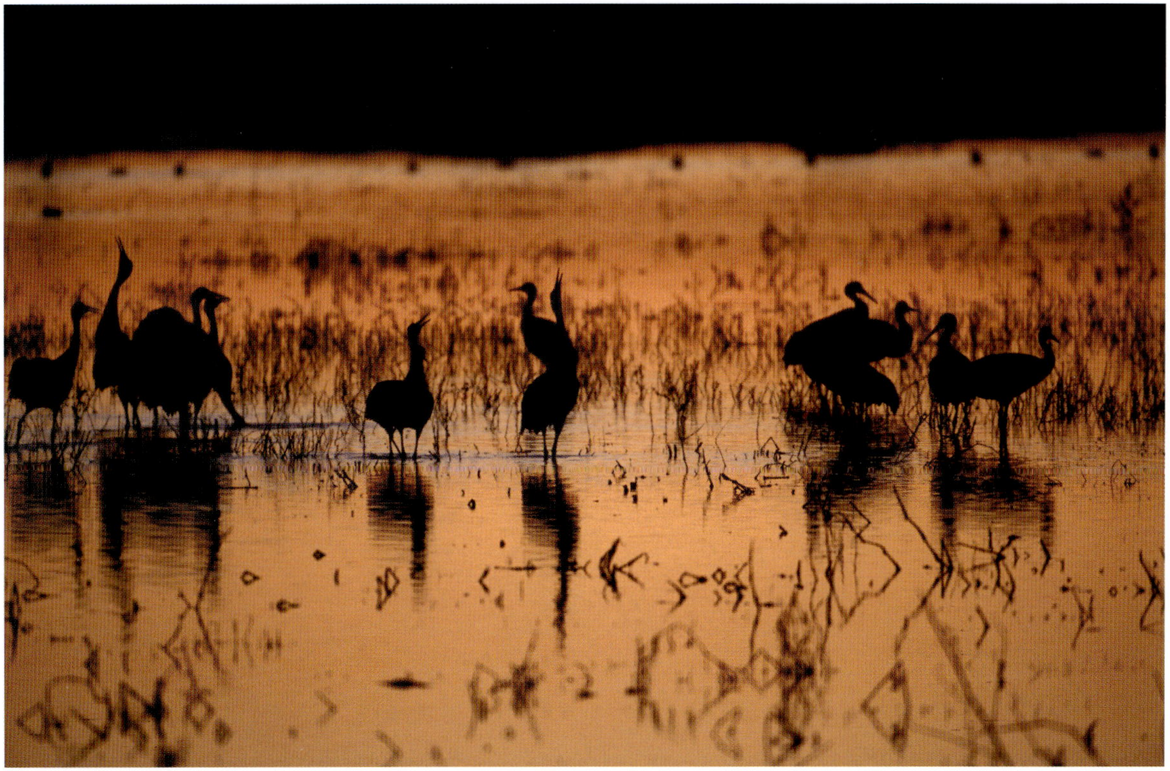

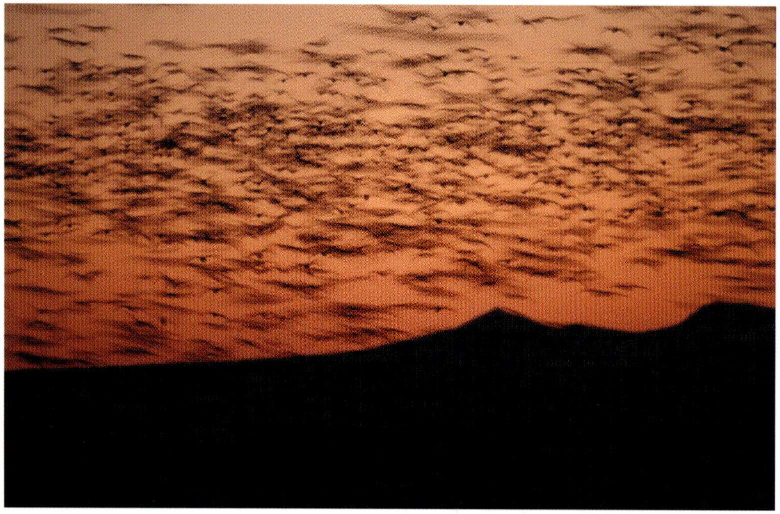

Left: As evening sets in, Snow Geese are on the move again - spooked by predators and looking to roost. Well outside the sensitivity of the film for available light, the birds blur the image in a fabulous swarm.

Right: A number of Snow Geese have settled in for the evening. In near constant motion, they soon vanish into the black New Mexico sky.

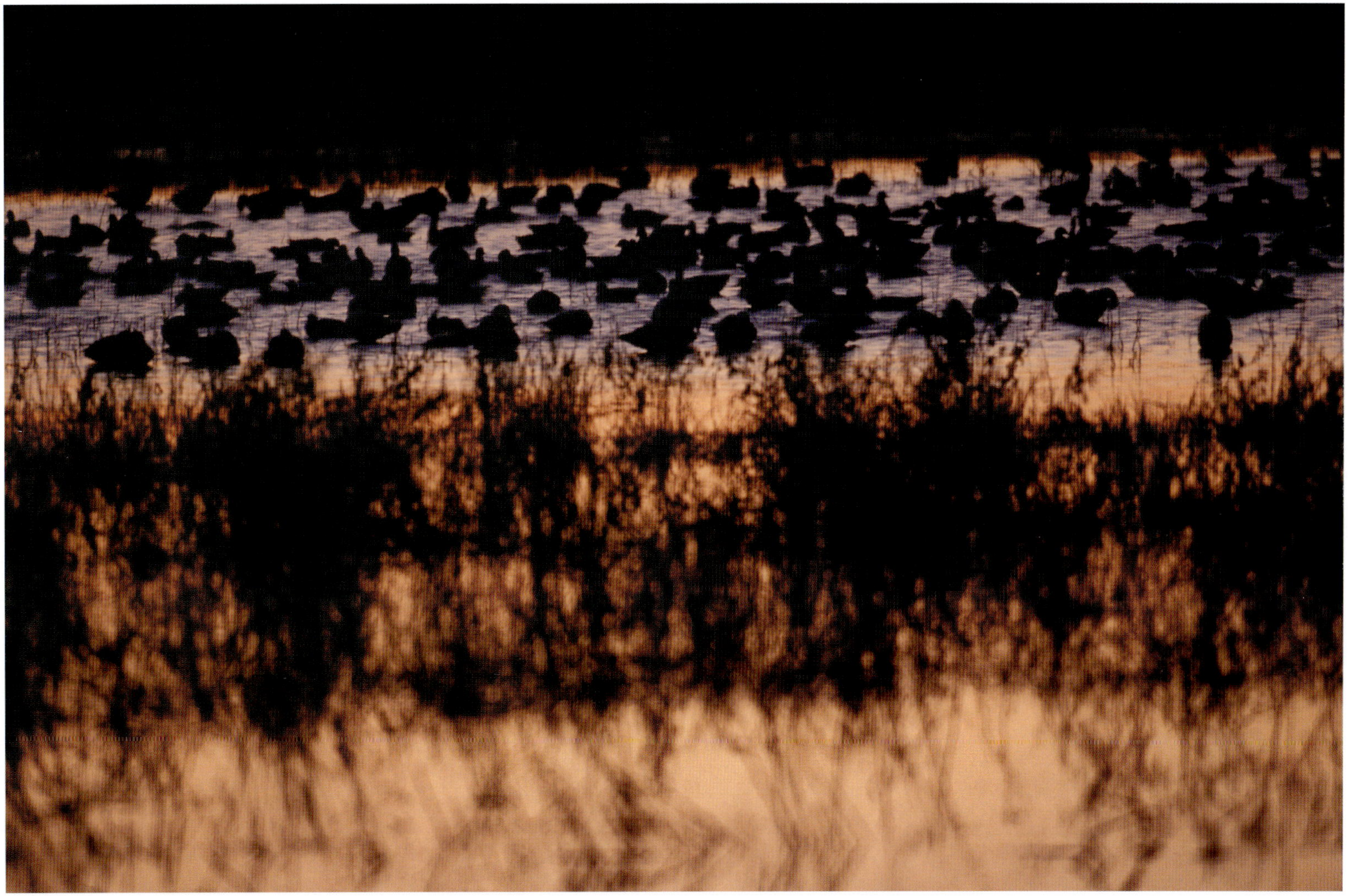

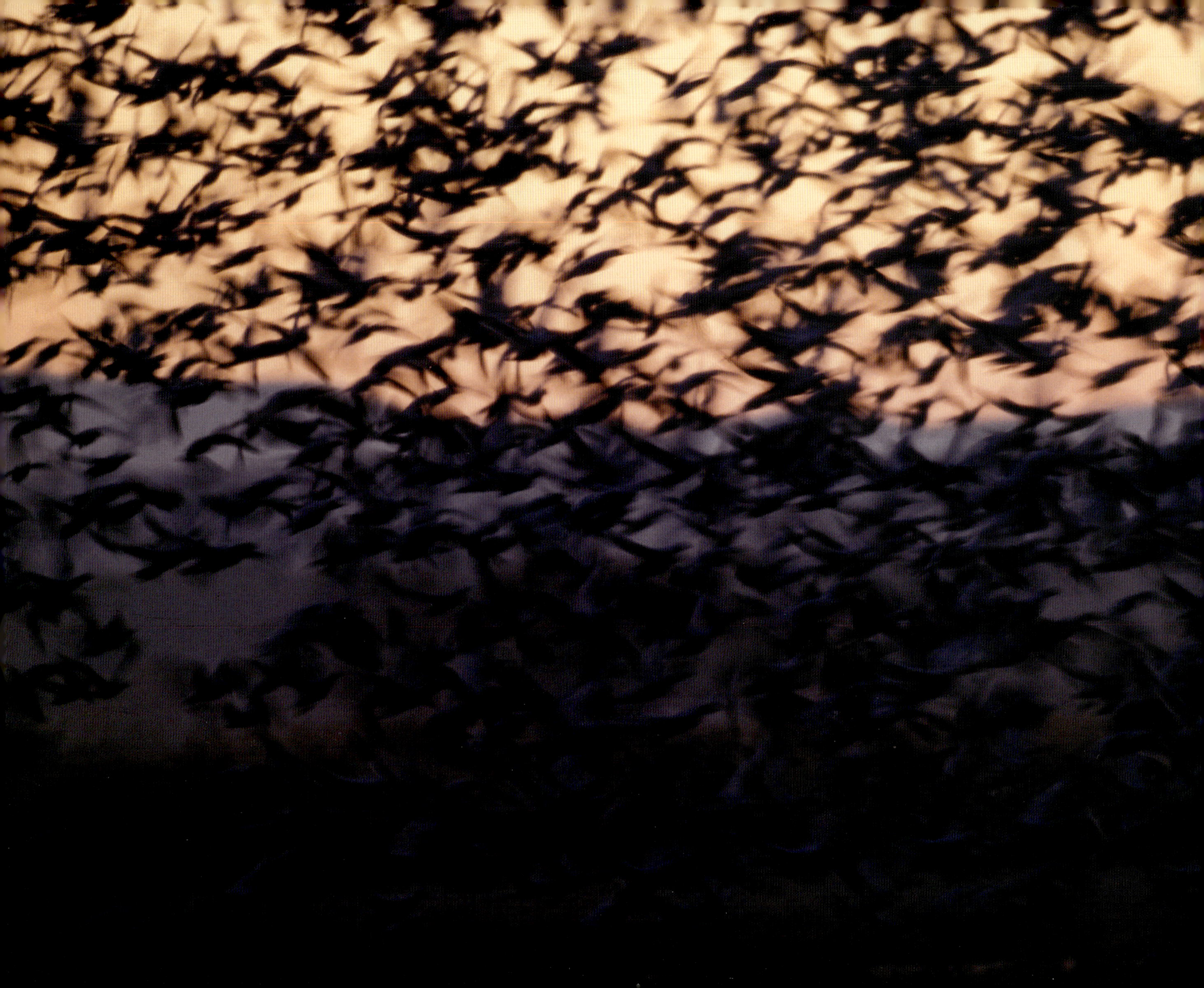

Left: Daybreak. Cold, frozen to the bone, and waiting for available light, the Snow Geese get an early start on the day. Thousands take to the air in an incredible and sudden event. The sound is loud, shocking, and confusing for first time visitors. As the flock bolts, the rhythm of the refuge is renewed.

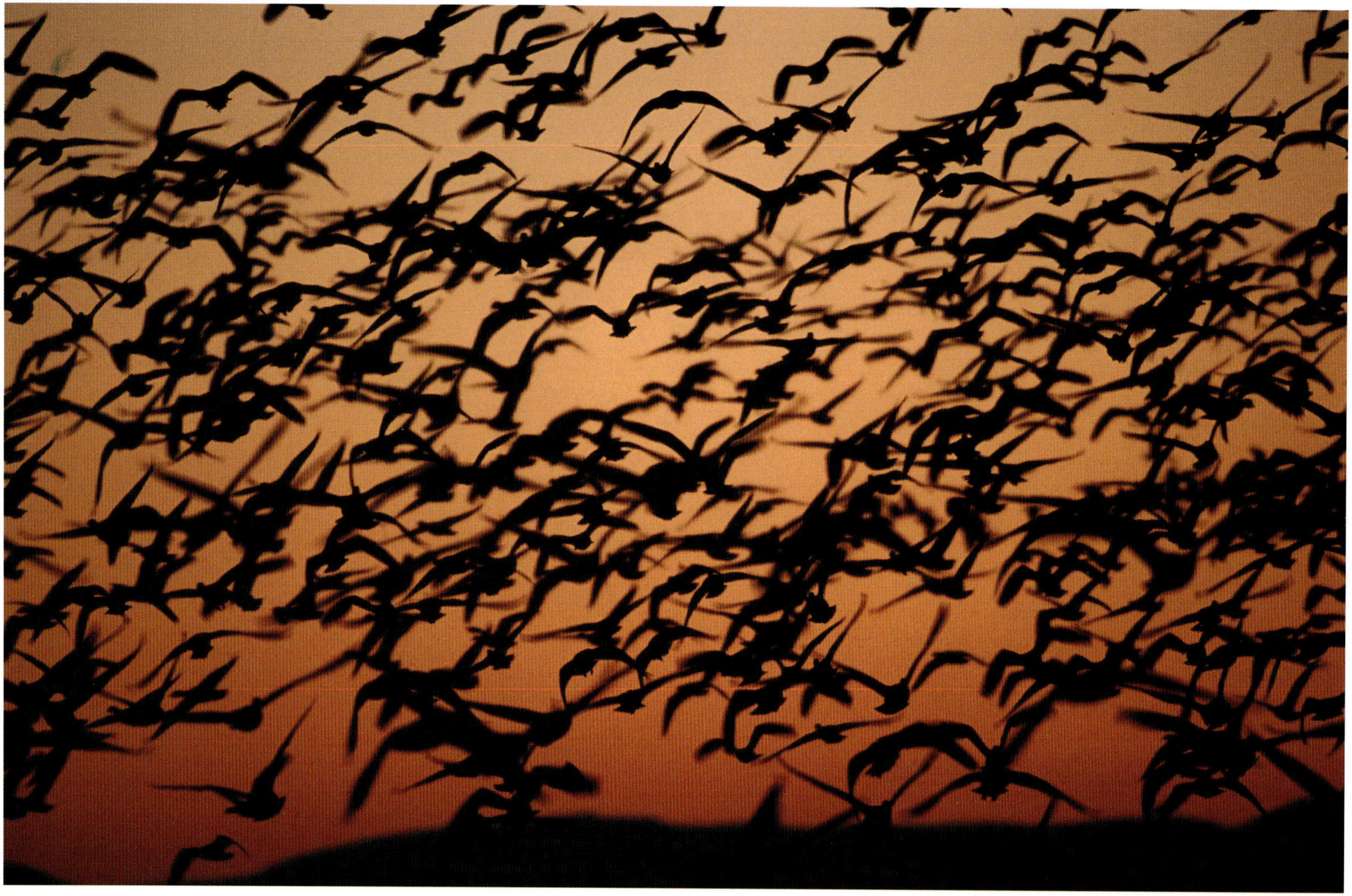

Above: At sunrise, the Snow Geese fly-out to feed on the cornfields in and around the refuge. Surrounded by the Chupadero Mountains on the west and the San Pascual Mountains on the east, Bosque del Apache is a welcomed refuge in an otherwise arid and barren climate.

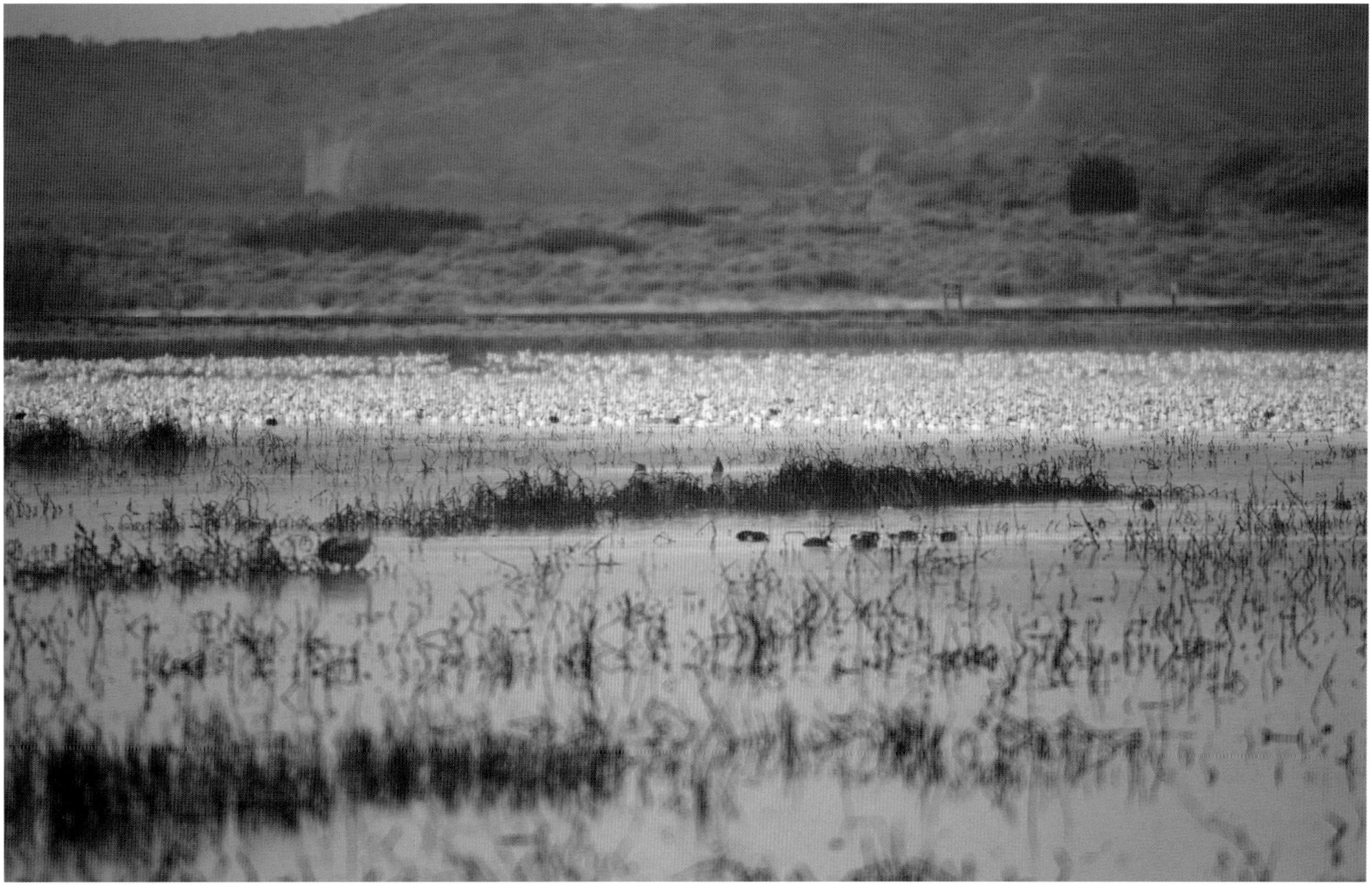

Above: First flying in from the farmlands on the northern side of the refuge, thousands are on the move. In early December the flock can exceed 30,000. In stages, off in the distance, thousands can be heard and seen airborne. In search of water, they vector in on the marsh surrounding the Flight Deck. Not there for long, they bolt again and again temporarily moving to the southwest.

Below: In smaller stages, less threatened, the geese gain altitude and move north. Unlike the dense flocks spooked into flight, long lines form in interwoven v-shaped flight patterns. Grace in flight, Bosque del Apache is a wonderful eco-system supporting species like Sandhill Cranes, Snow Geese, and raptors to flourish.

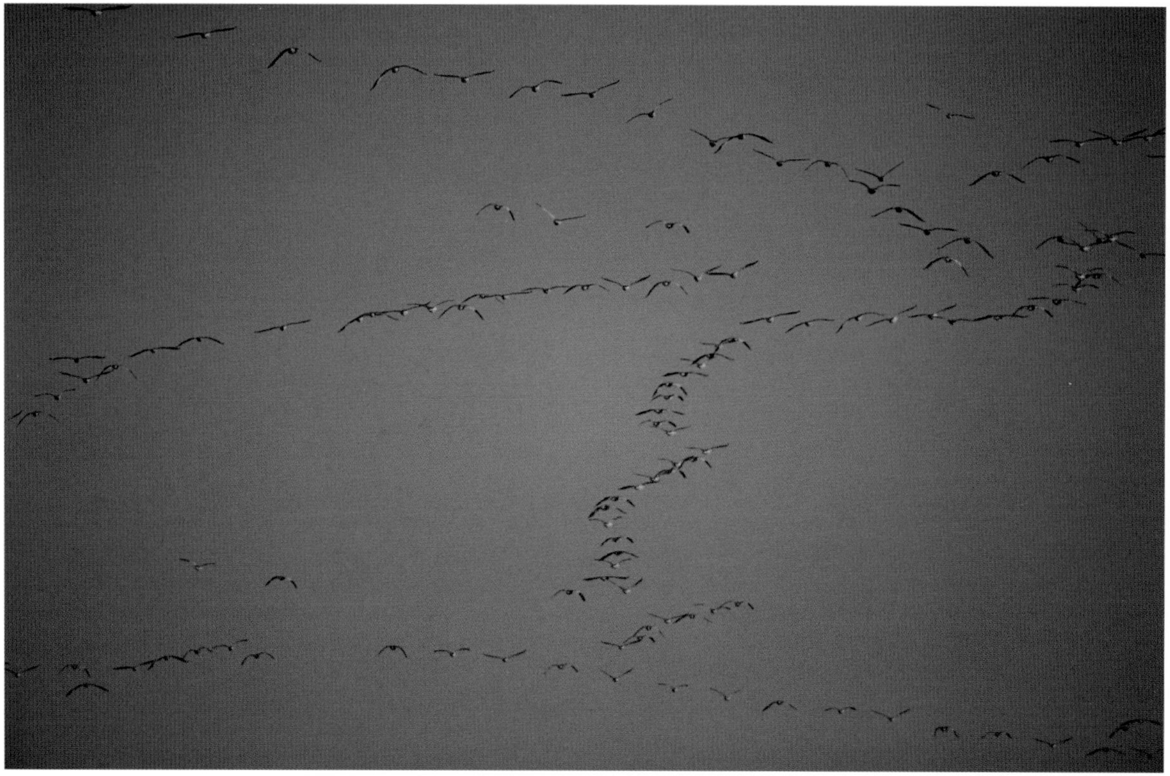

Below: Flying along the Chupadero Mountain ranges, the geese quickly leave the marsh waters of the Flight Deck to warm in the sun, feed in the farmlands, and start the new day.

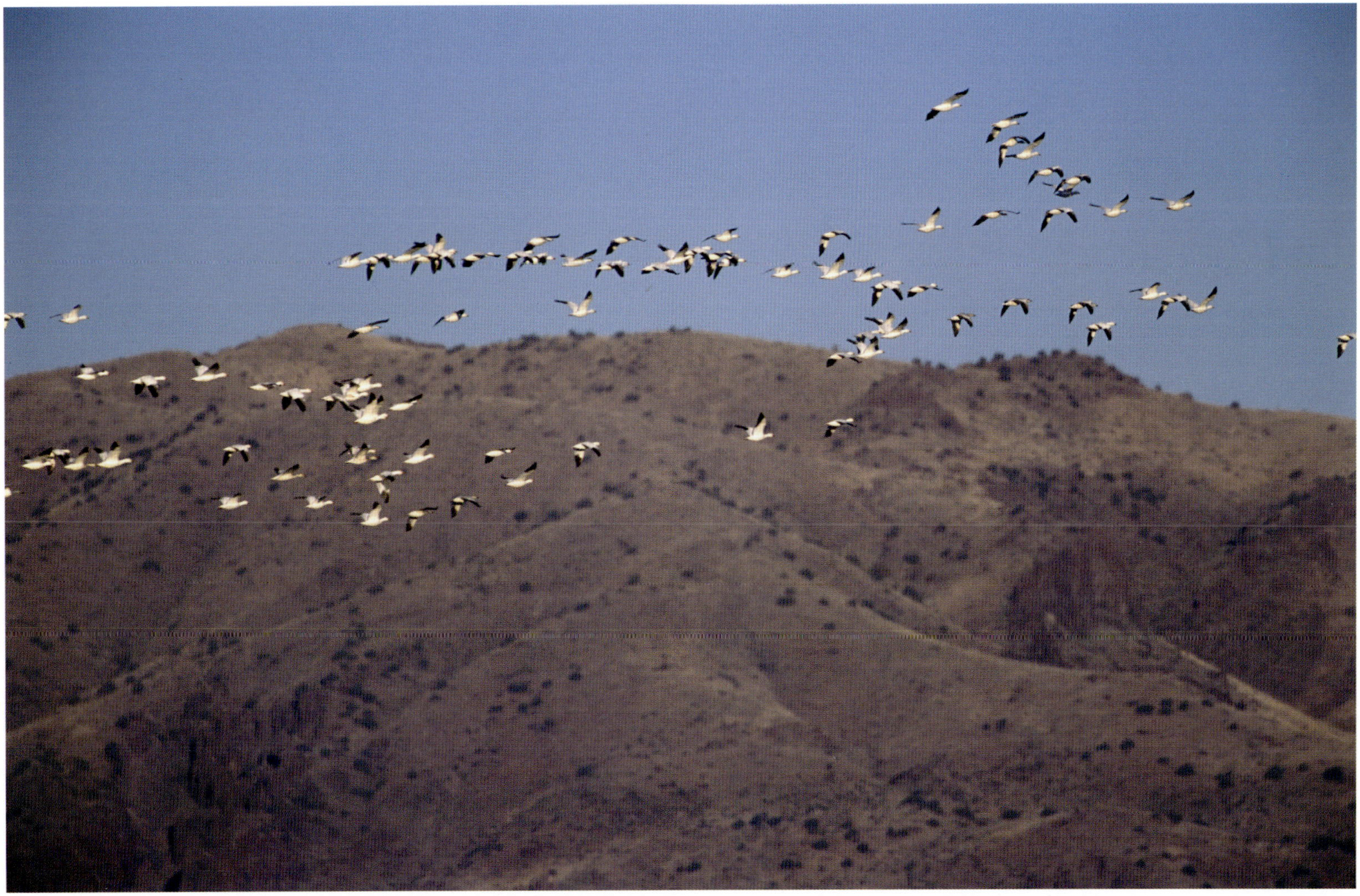

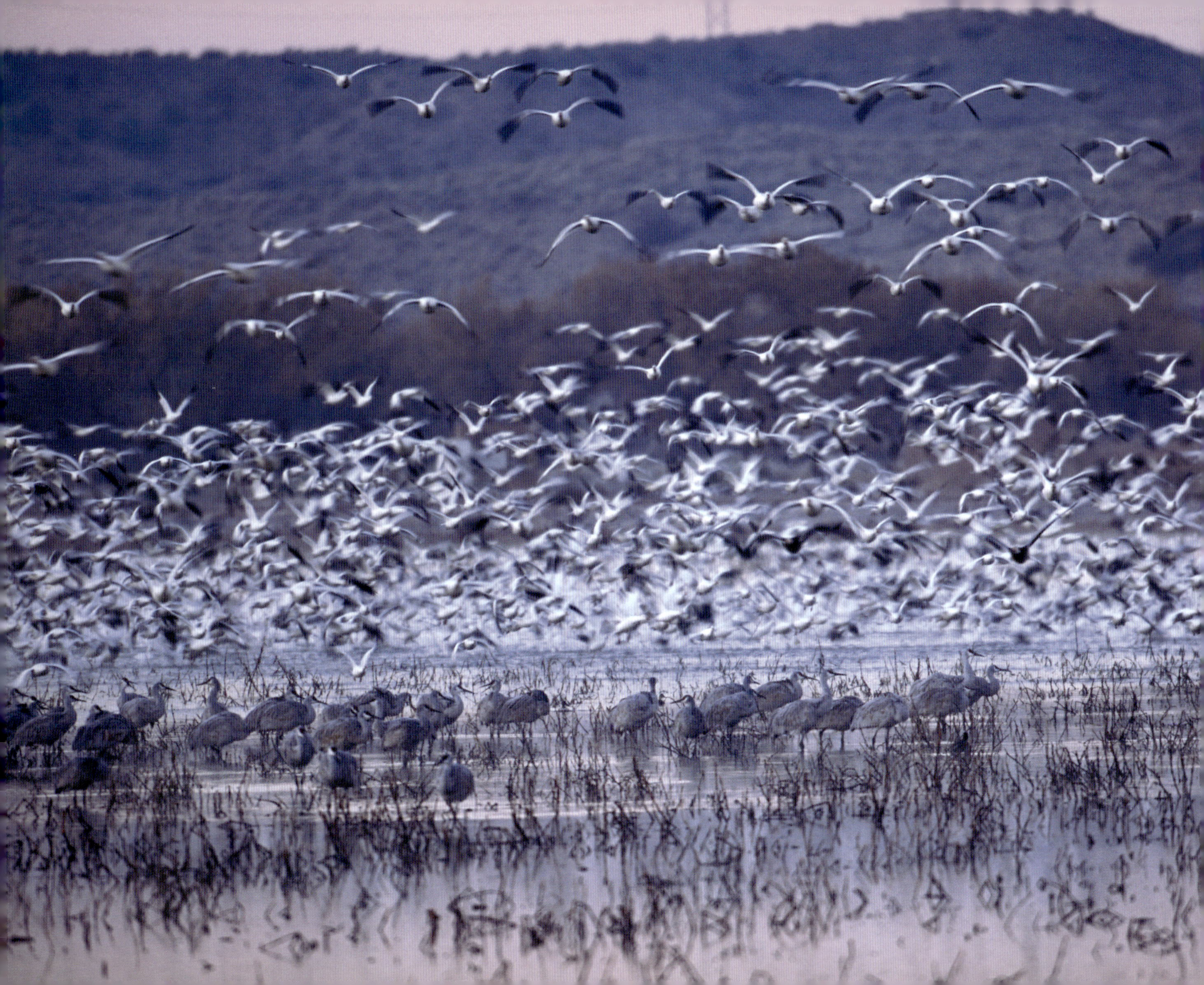

Left: Wave after wave the geese take to the air. Still awakening from the night, the Sandhill Cranes remain stationary, casually observing all the commotion.

Right: Against a colorful morning sky, the geese continue to form long chains spreading out in magnificent threads of life. The white plumage of the Snow Geese is critical for survival in the breeding grounds of the Canadian Arctic and is a perfect match for the colorful New Mexico sky.

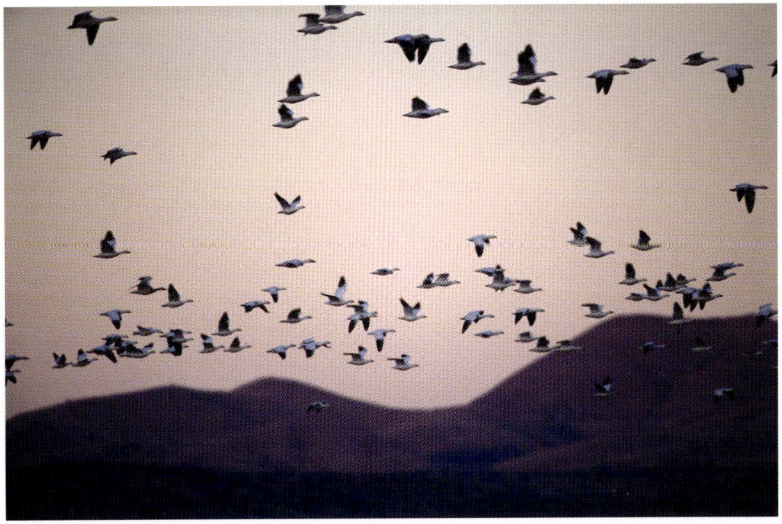

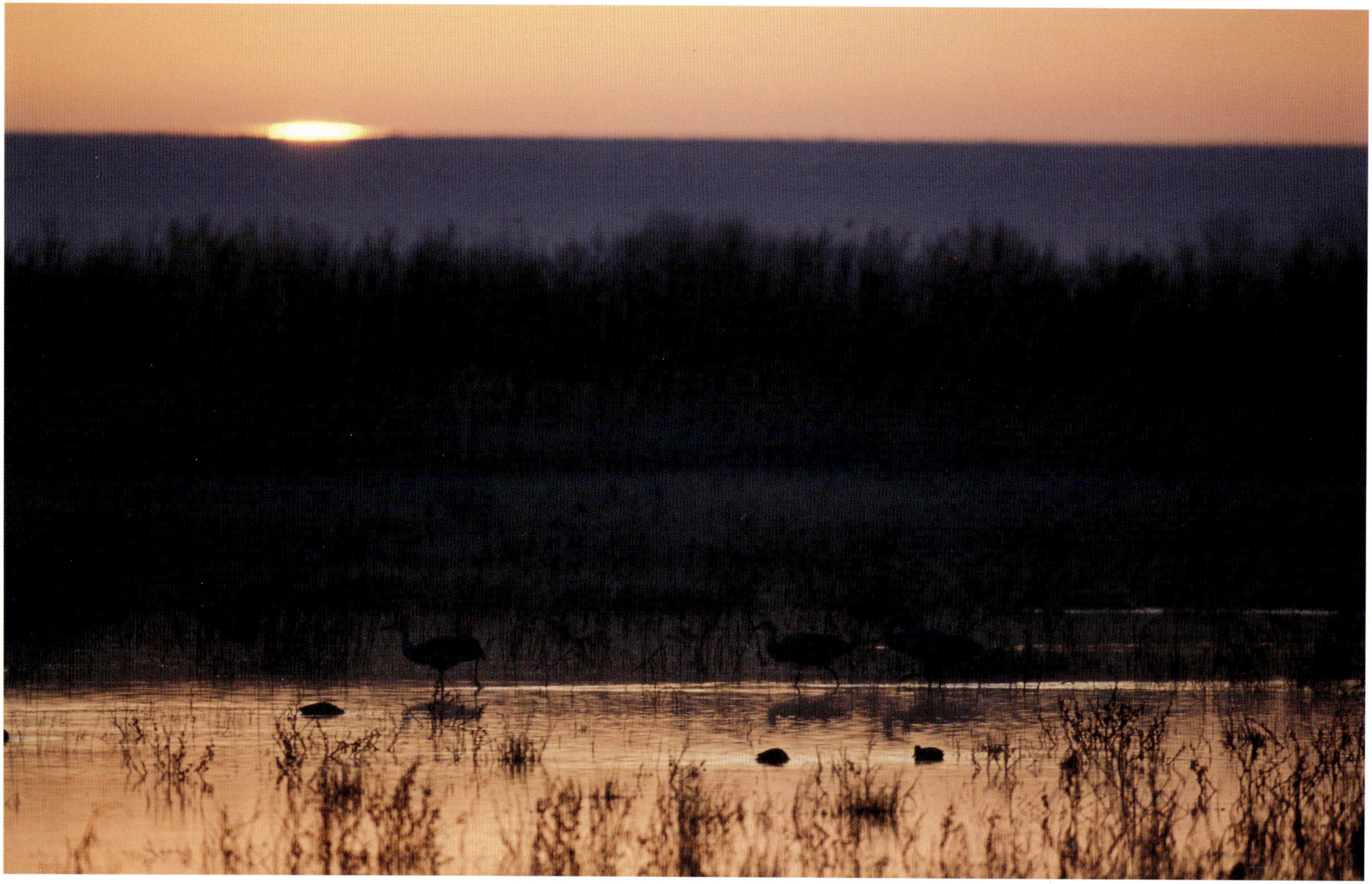

Left: Finally, with the geese on the move, the sun breaks over the mountains in the distance. Silhouettes of cranes, as in the evening, once again are on the move.

Right: All across the refuge, wildlife is on the move. Established in 1939 as a national wildlife refuge, Bosque del Apache today supports species such as cranes and geese to thrive while the brutal winter of the north is underway.

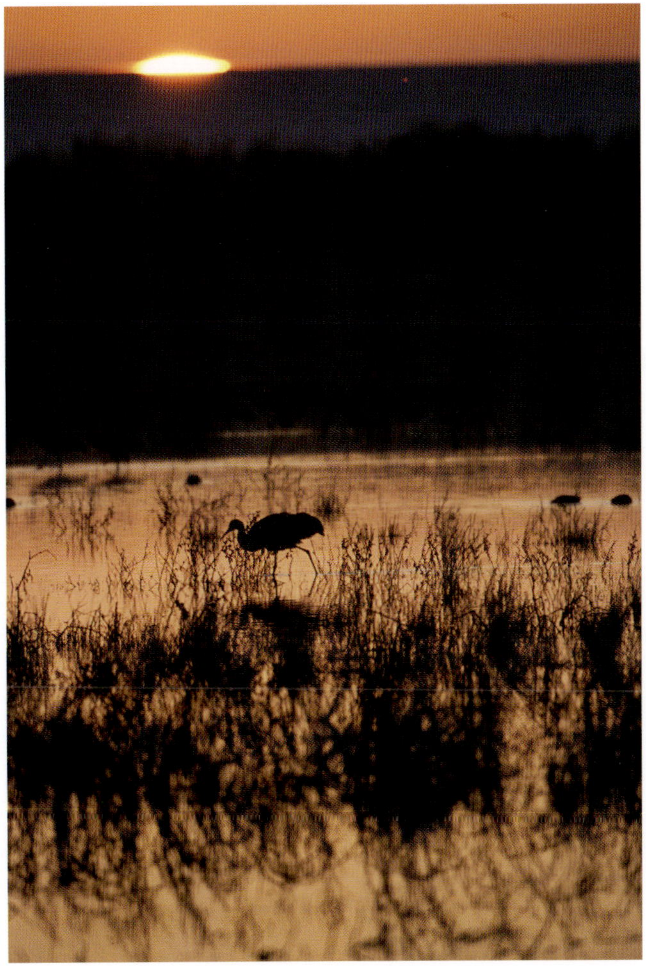

Right: In the warmth of the winter sun, the cranes stretch their wings in preparation for flight. No hurry here.

Below: Some still sleeping, others on watch, they awake from their roost to a cold New Mexico morning.

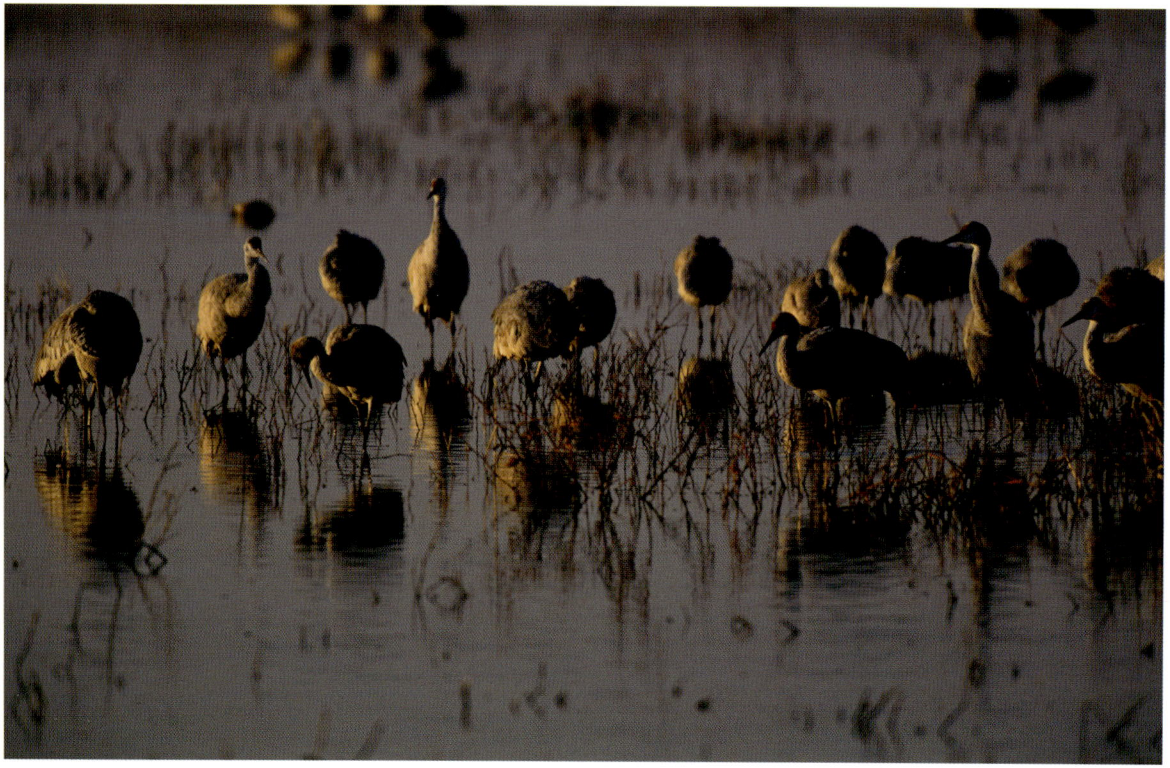

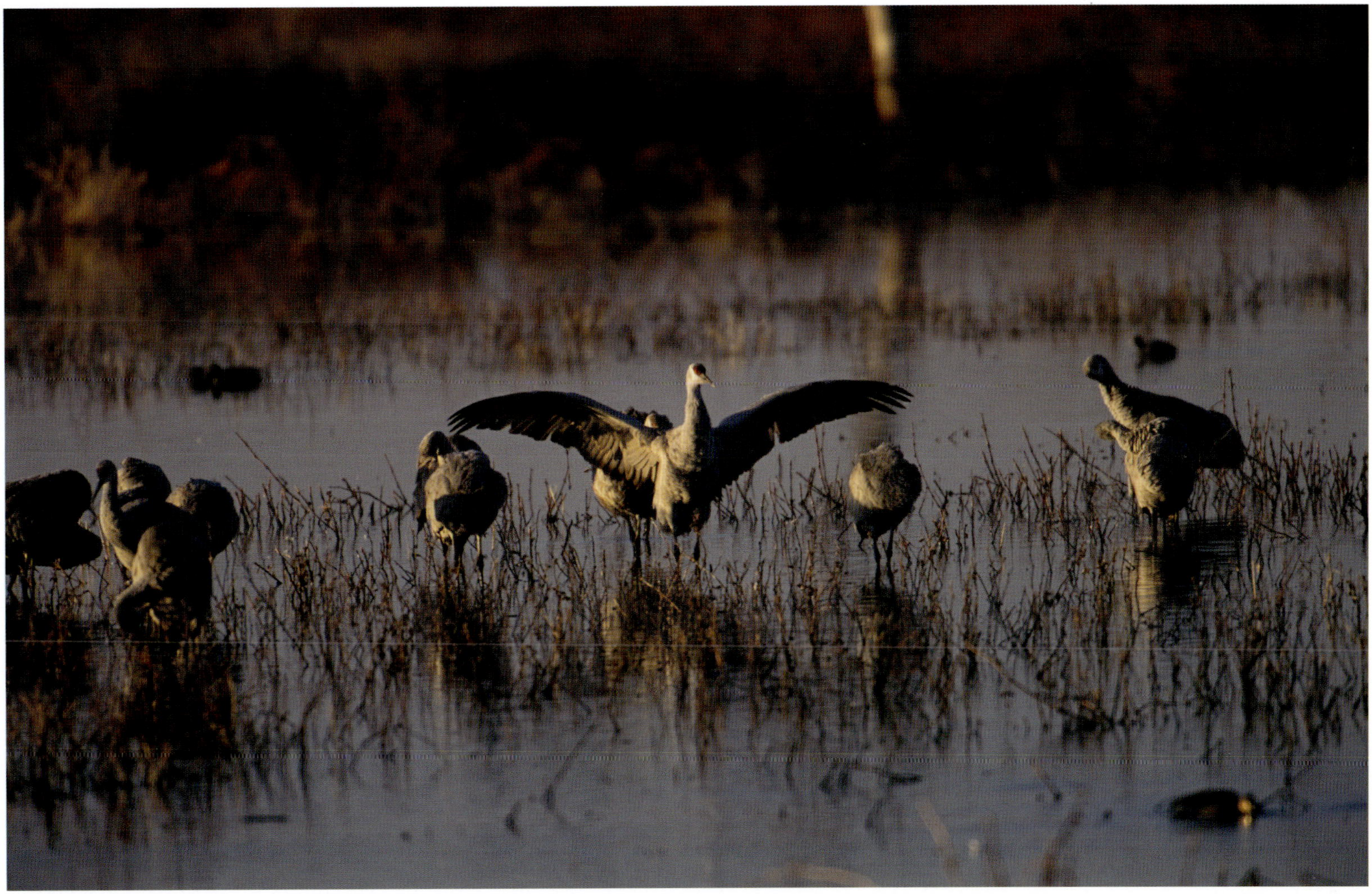

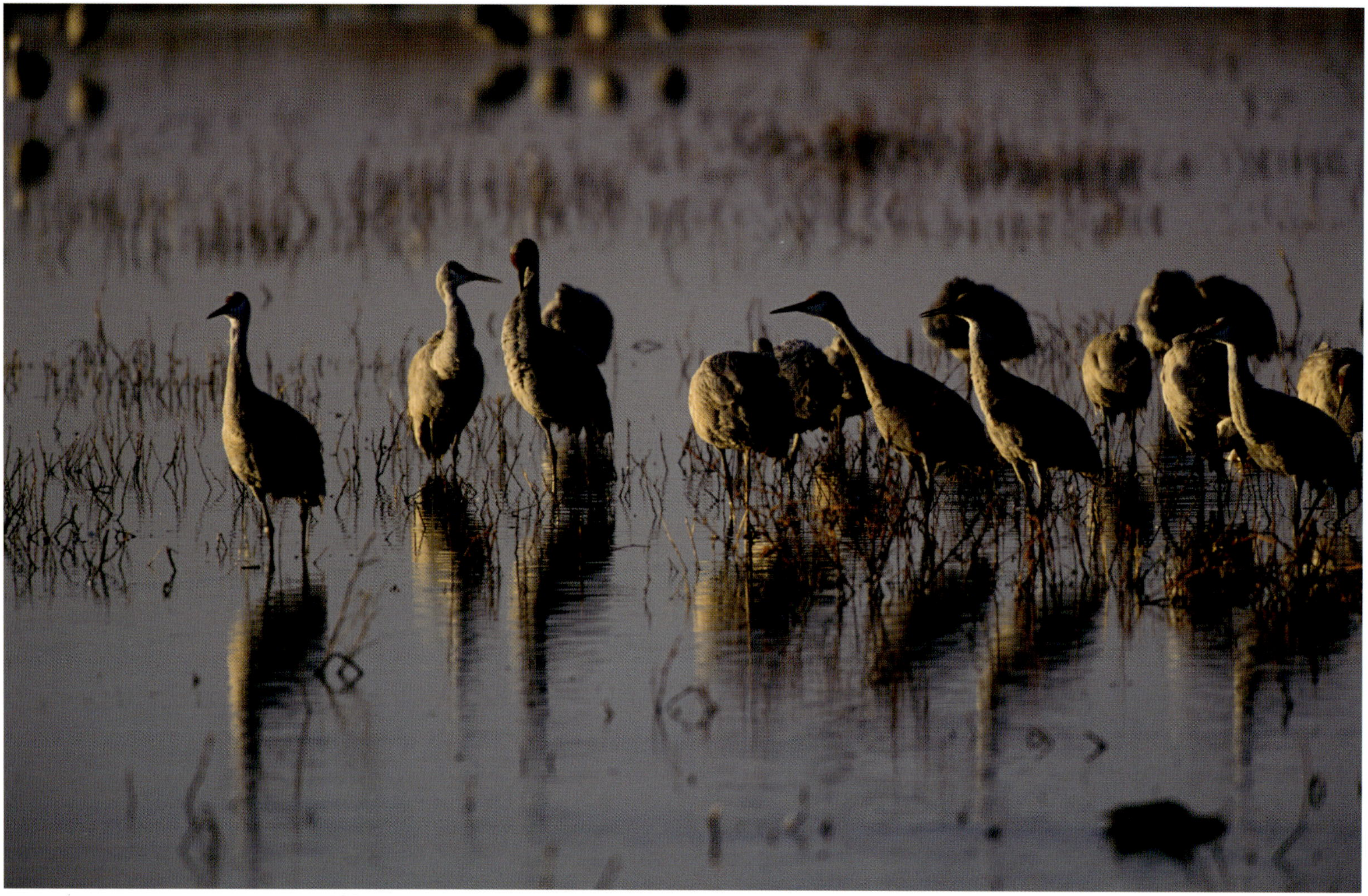

Above: With the sun up, several cranes contemplate flight. Stretching their necks in the direction of take-off, they visually signaling to the flock and take up the launching position. Within seconds the first flight of the new day is on.

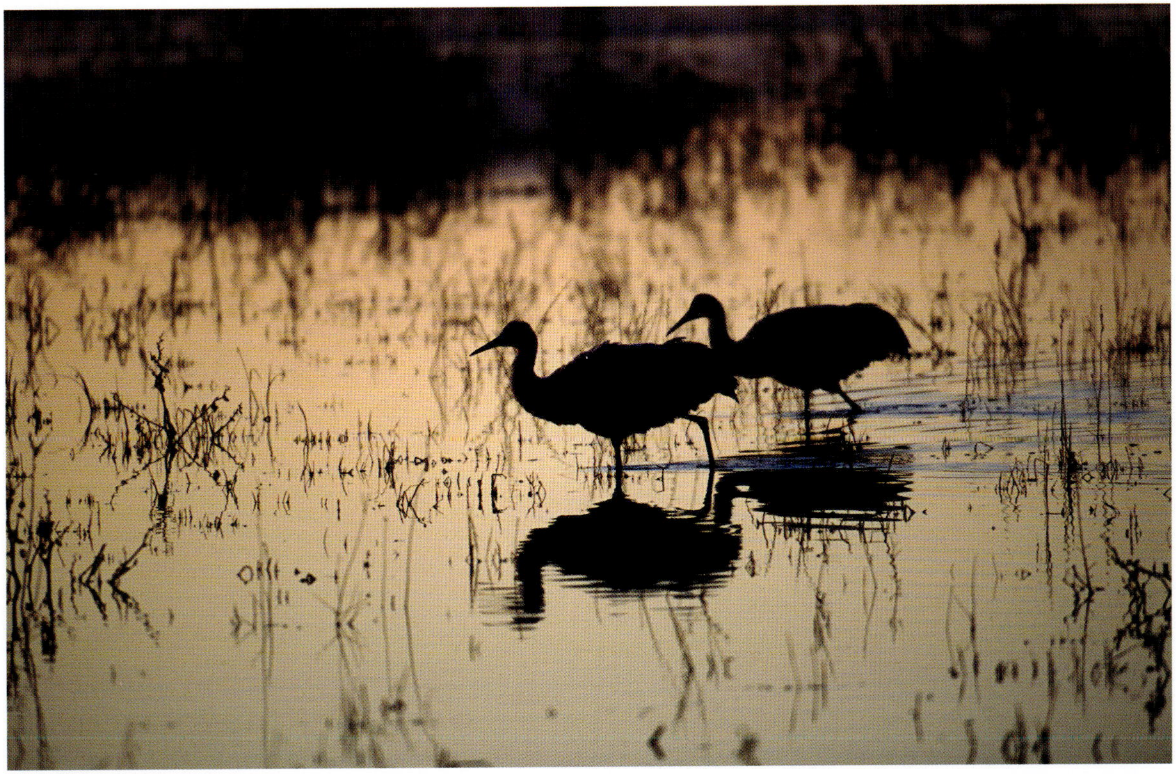

Left: Some take to the air, others are on the move as the sunrise continues to deepen in intensity.

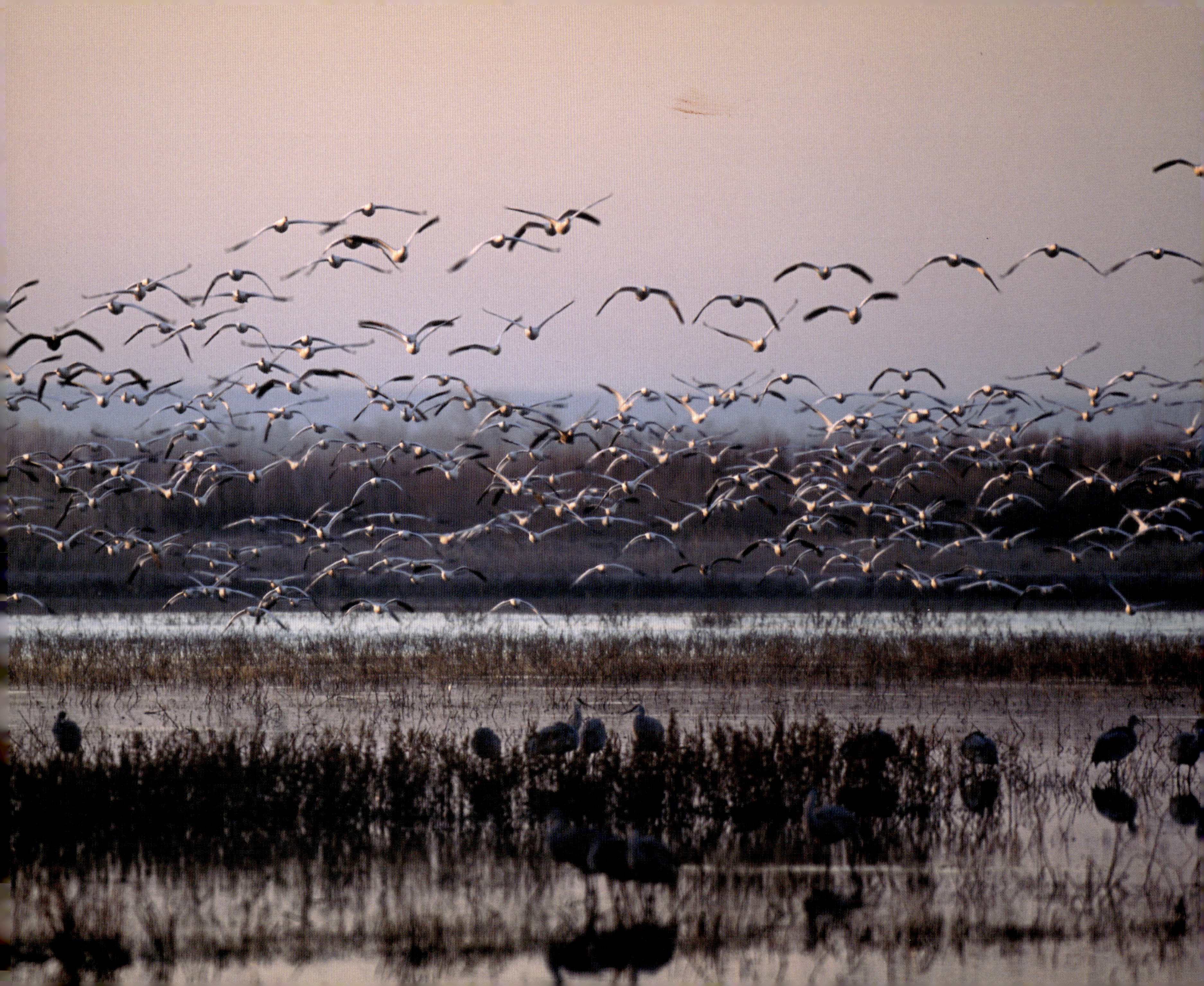

Left: In one final wave, the Snow Geese leave the Flight Deck observation area. Not far behind, a lone eagle is riding low and fast. Now there is real motivation to be moving.

Below: Sweeping waves and long lines of birds move in a constant rhythm of flight.

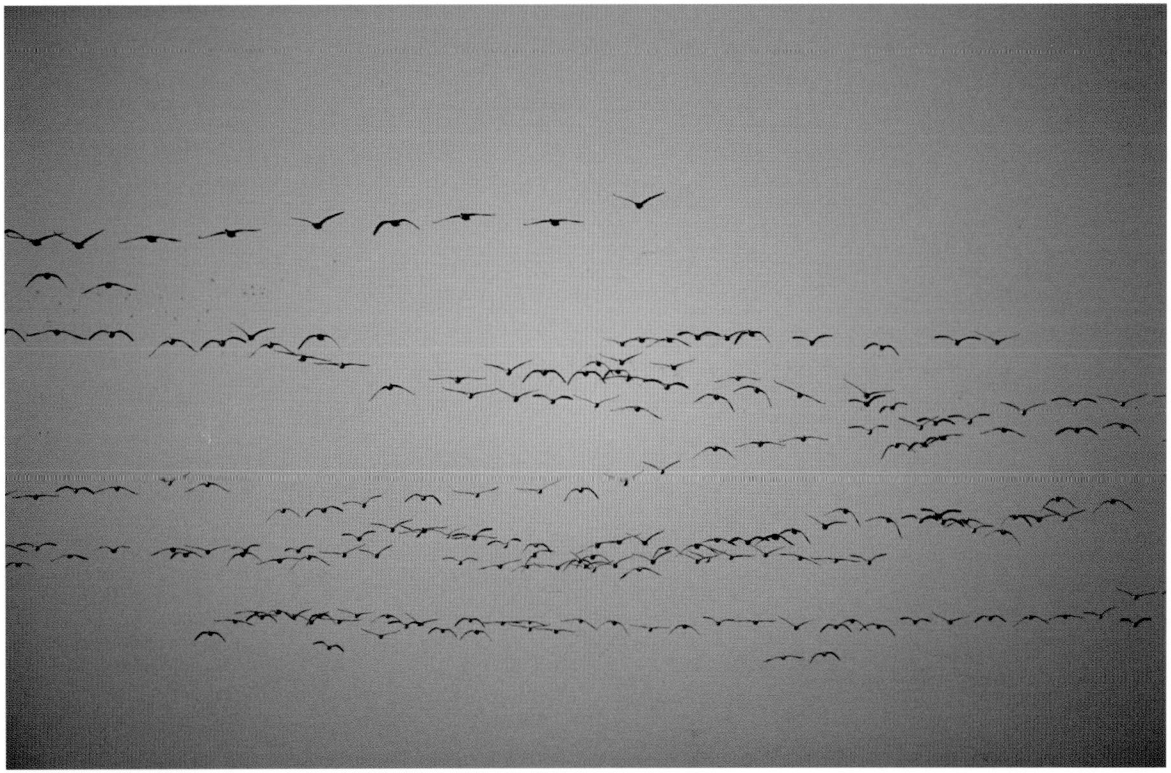

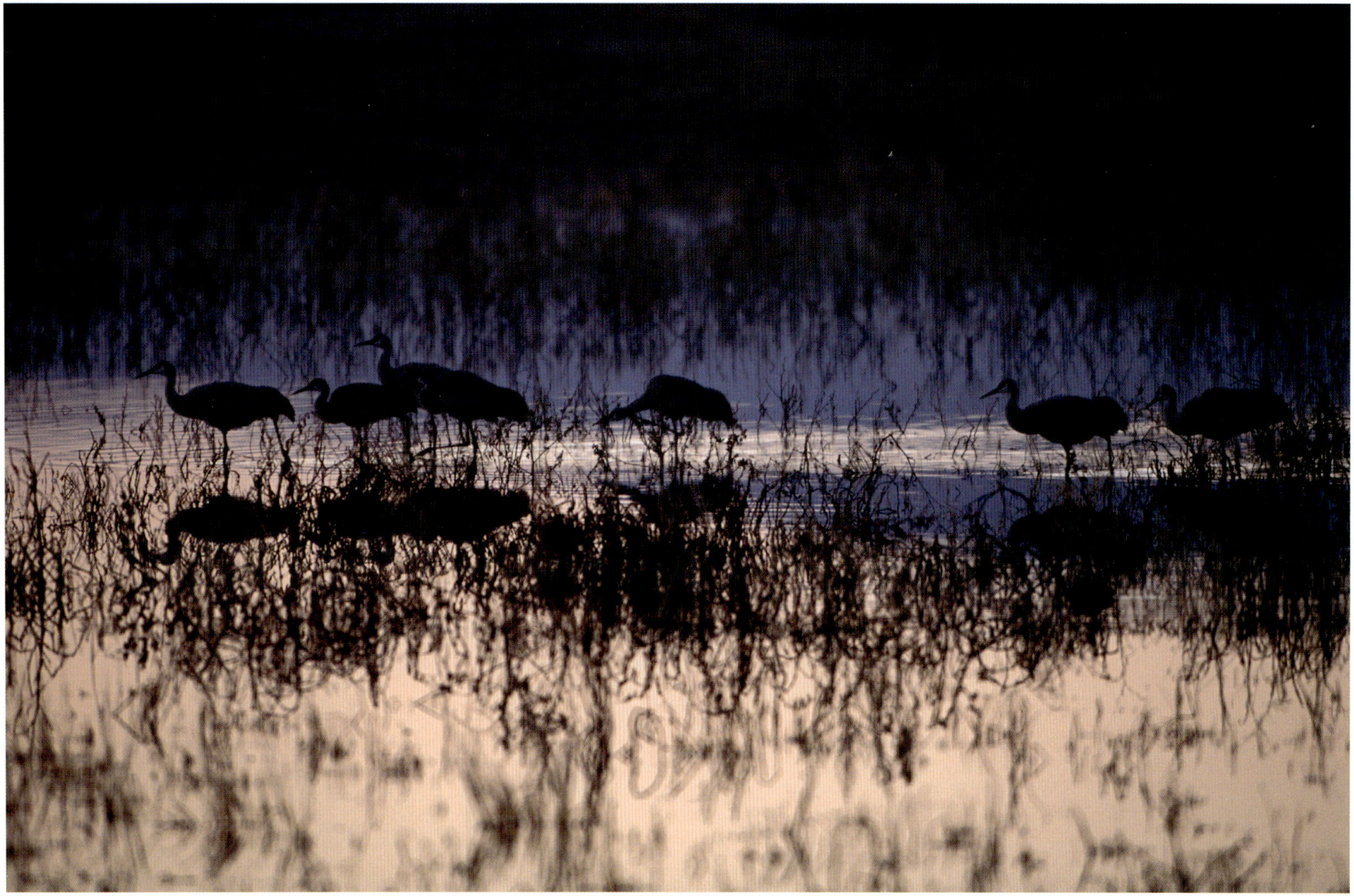

Above: A leader forms up a group of sandhills. Stretching, preening, and scratching, the cranes get ready for another day.

Below: Distant clouds reflect the strong, colorful New Mexico sunrise. Heading out to feed, the geese gain altitude.

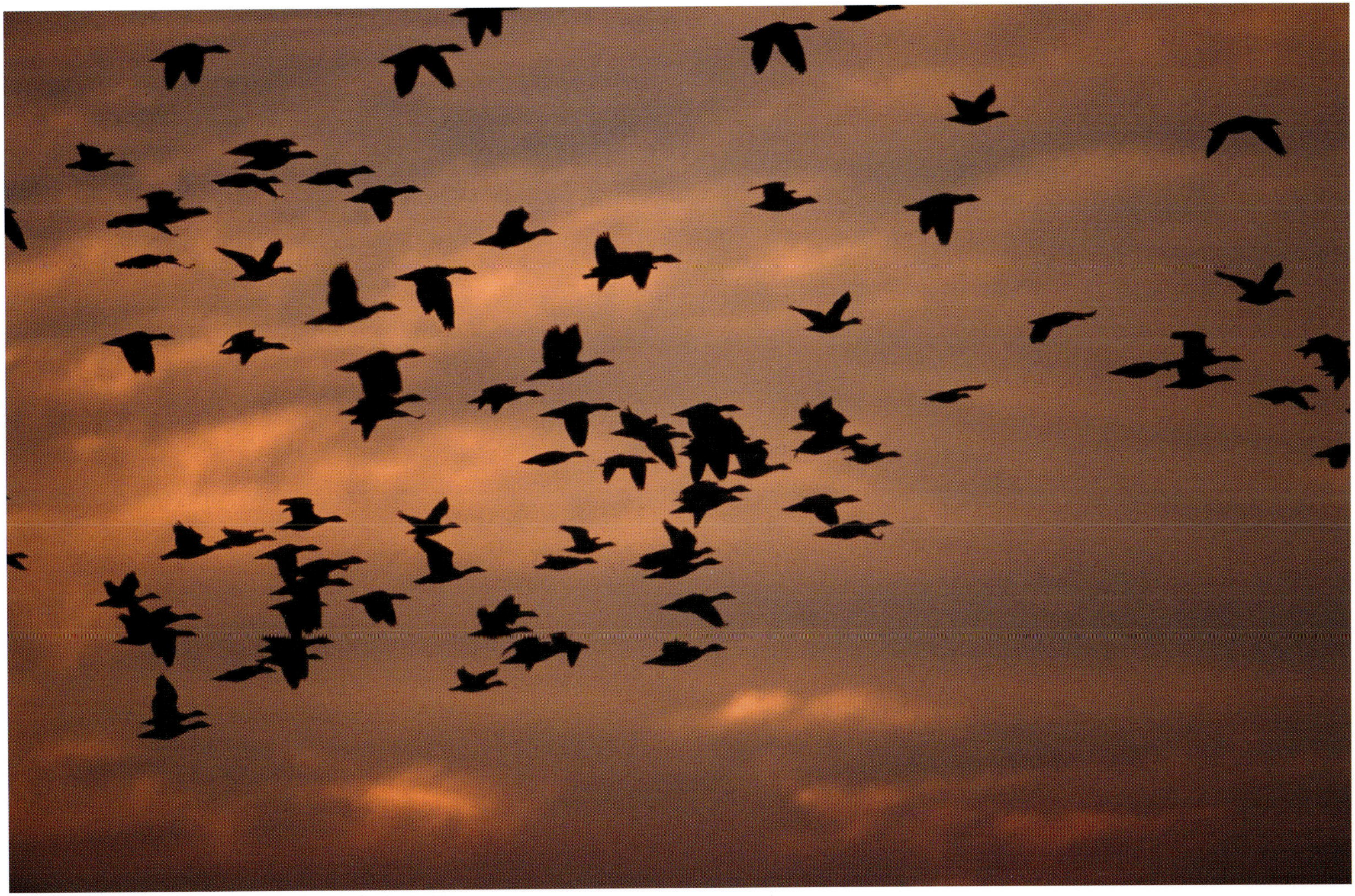

Below: The strongest lead an undulating chain of followers. Thousands have taken to the air. As the sunlight gets stronger, the geese appear more distant. Time to move on.

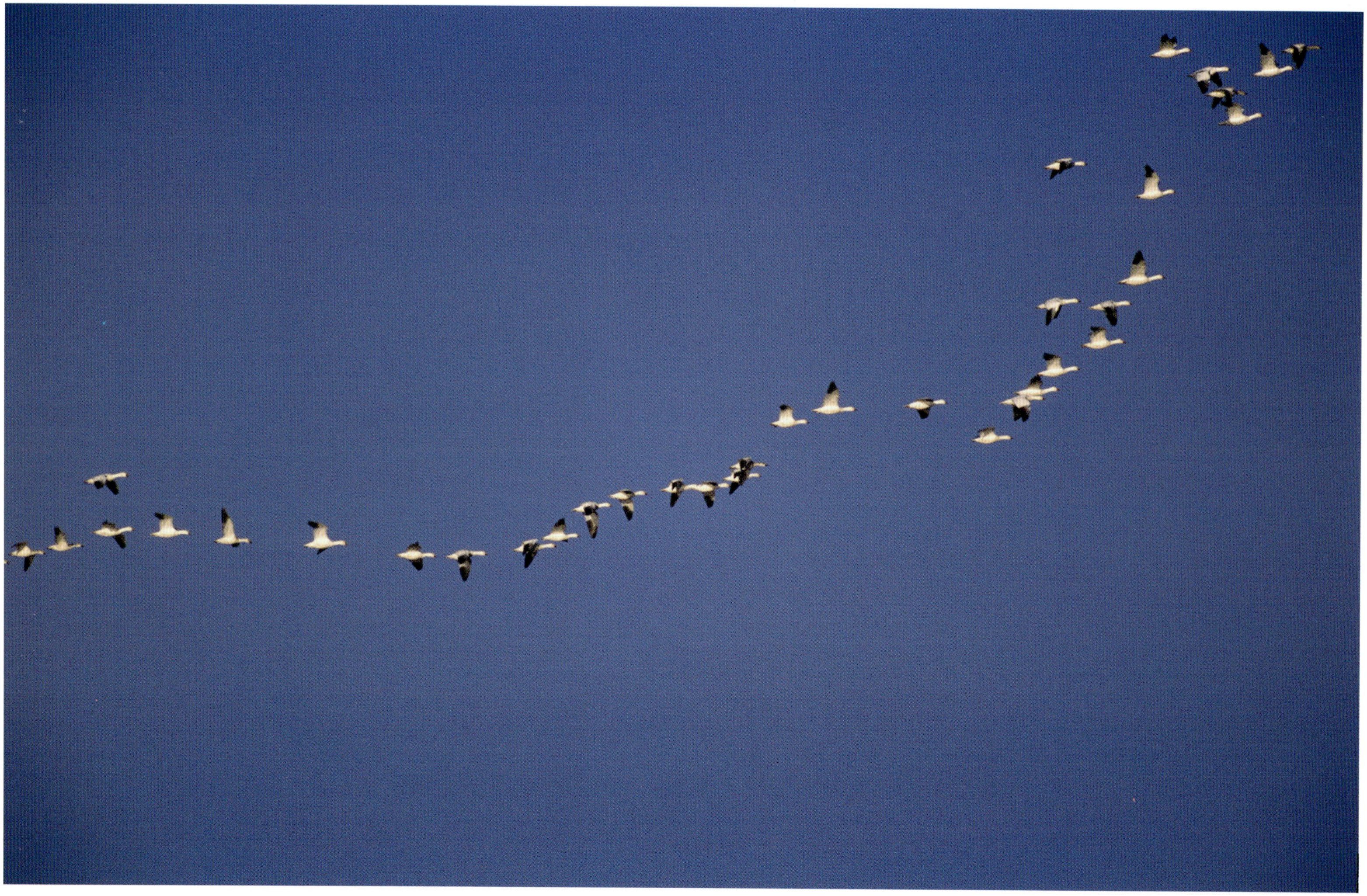

Right: As the geese fly-out of the marshes, wildlife throughout the refuge become visible. This male Ring-necked Pheasant calls out while showing his vibrant plumage.

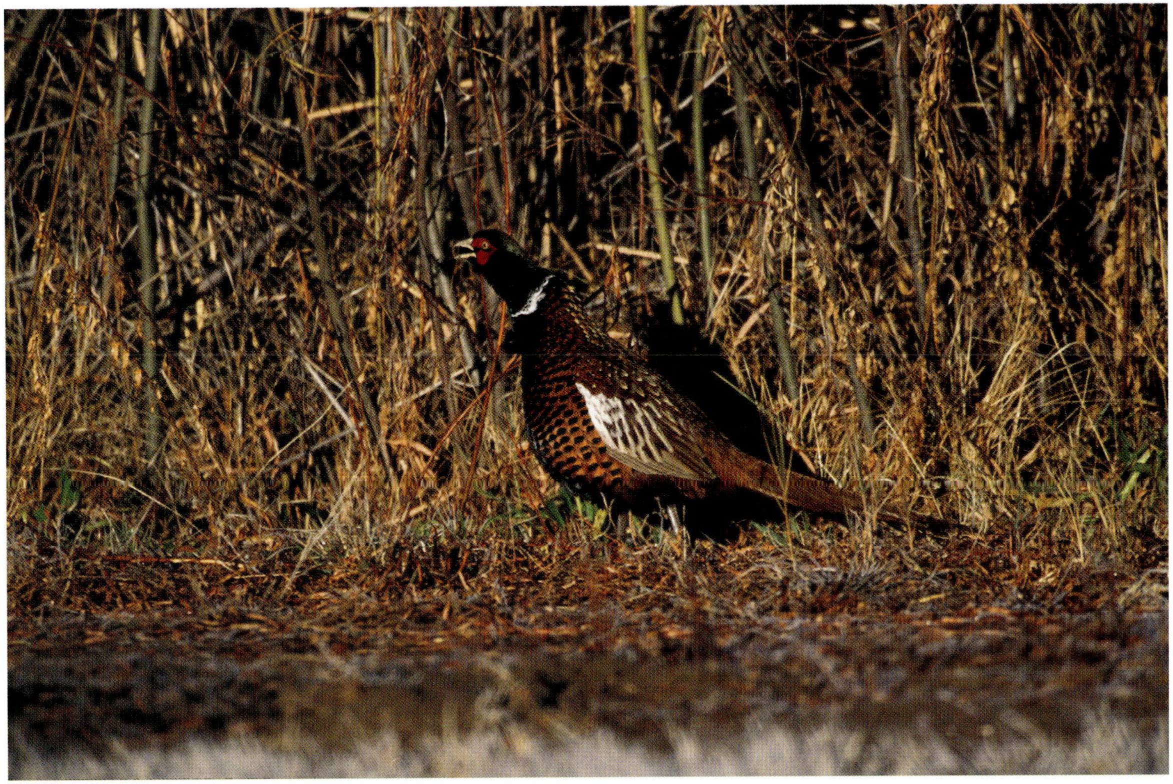

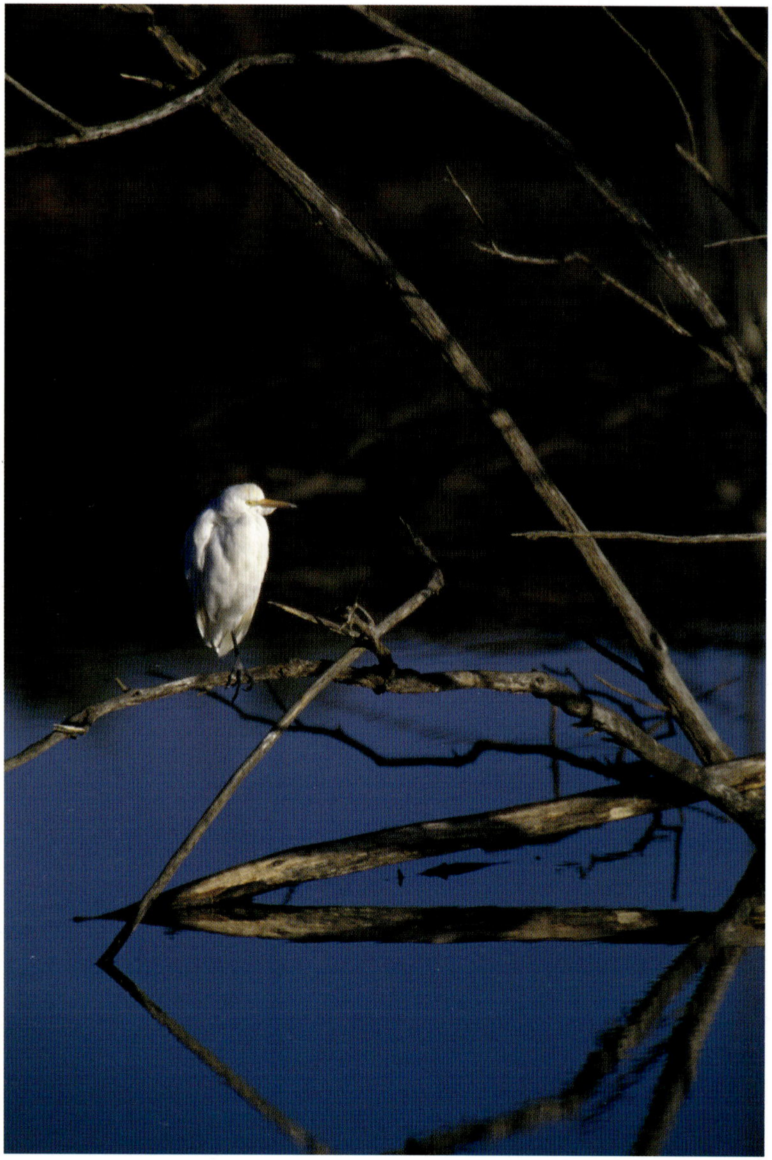

Left: On a quiet pond, a Snowy Egret awakens from roost. With its slender bill and black legs, this egret is easily spooked from the auto route.

Right: Shortly down the road, a Cooper's Hawk takes up a position overlooking the vast fields and marshlands of Bosque del Apache.

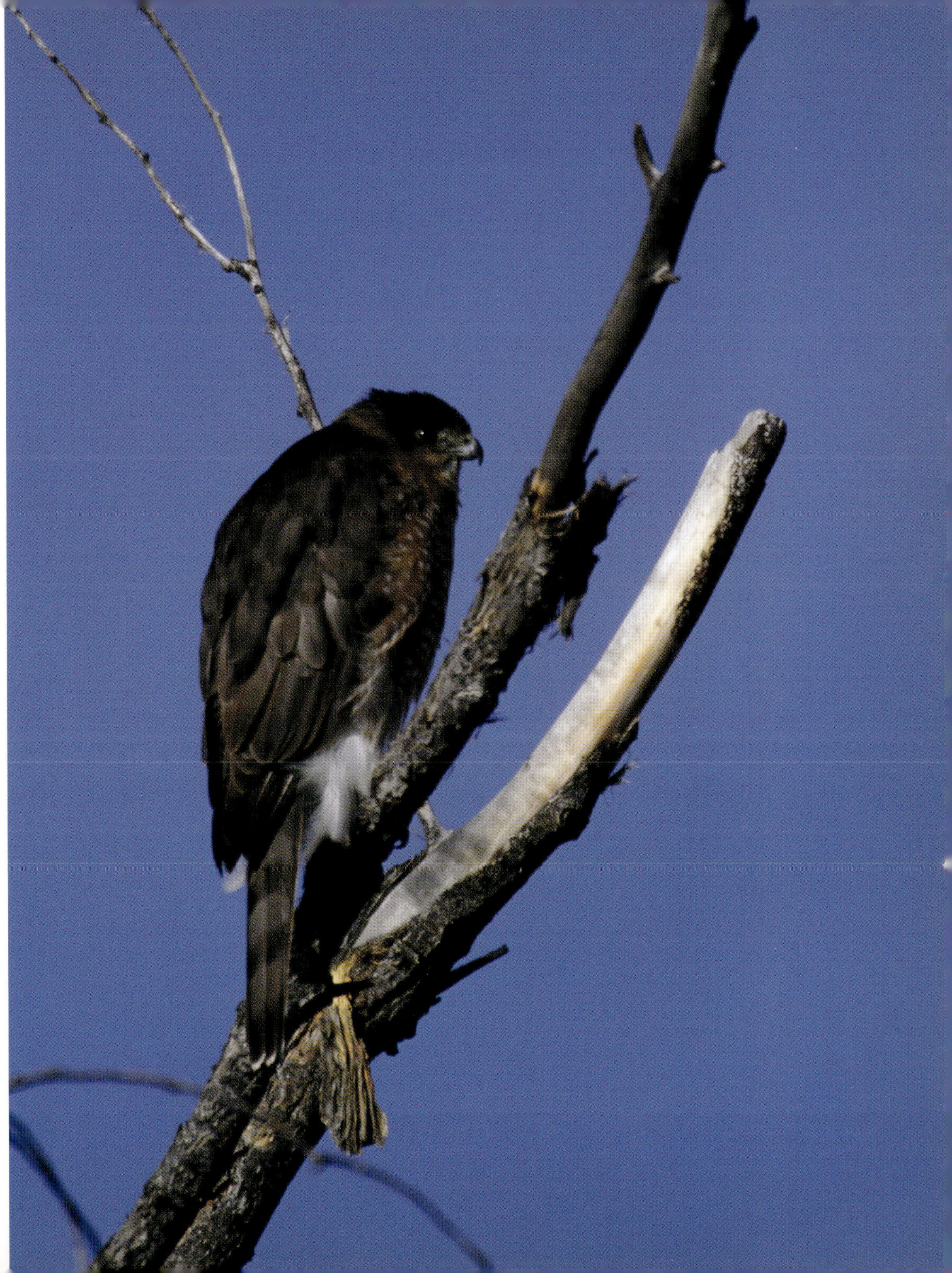

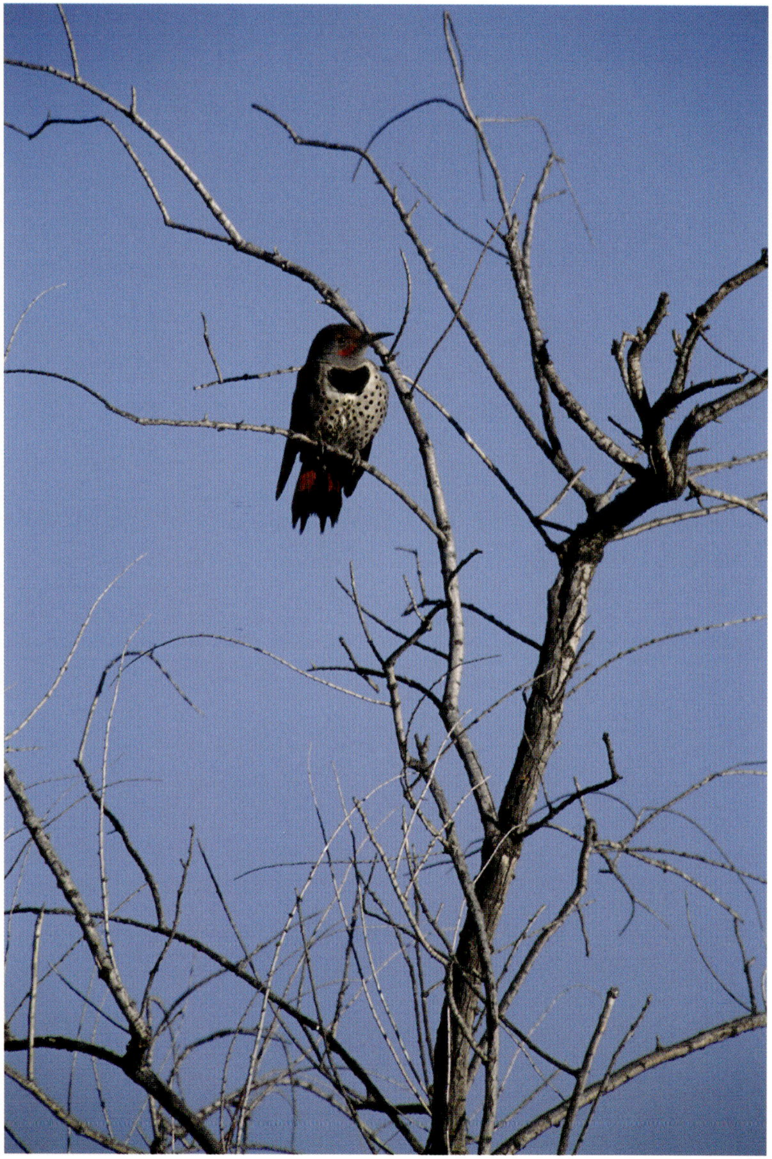

Left: Northern Flickers can be seen perching across Bosque del Apache in the morning hours.

Right: Likewise, numerous raptors take up positions in the trees lining the fields and marshes.

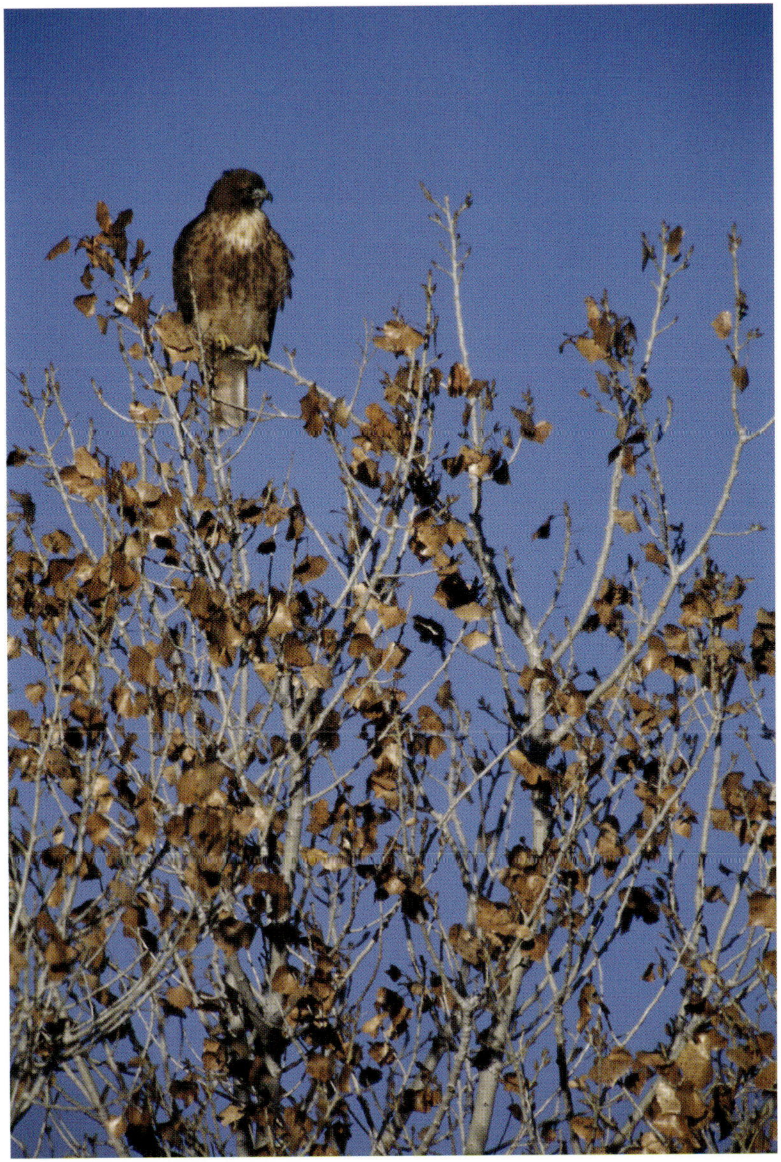

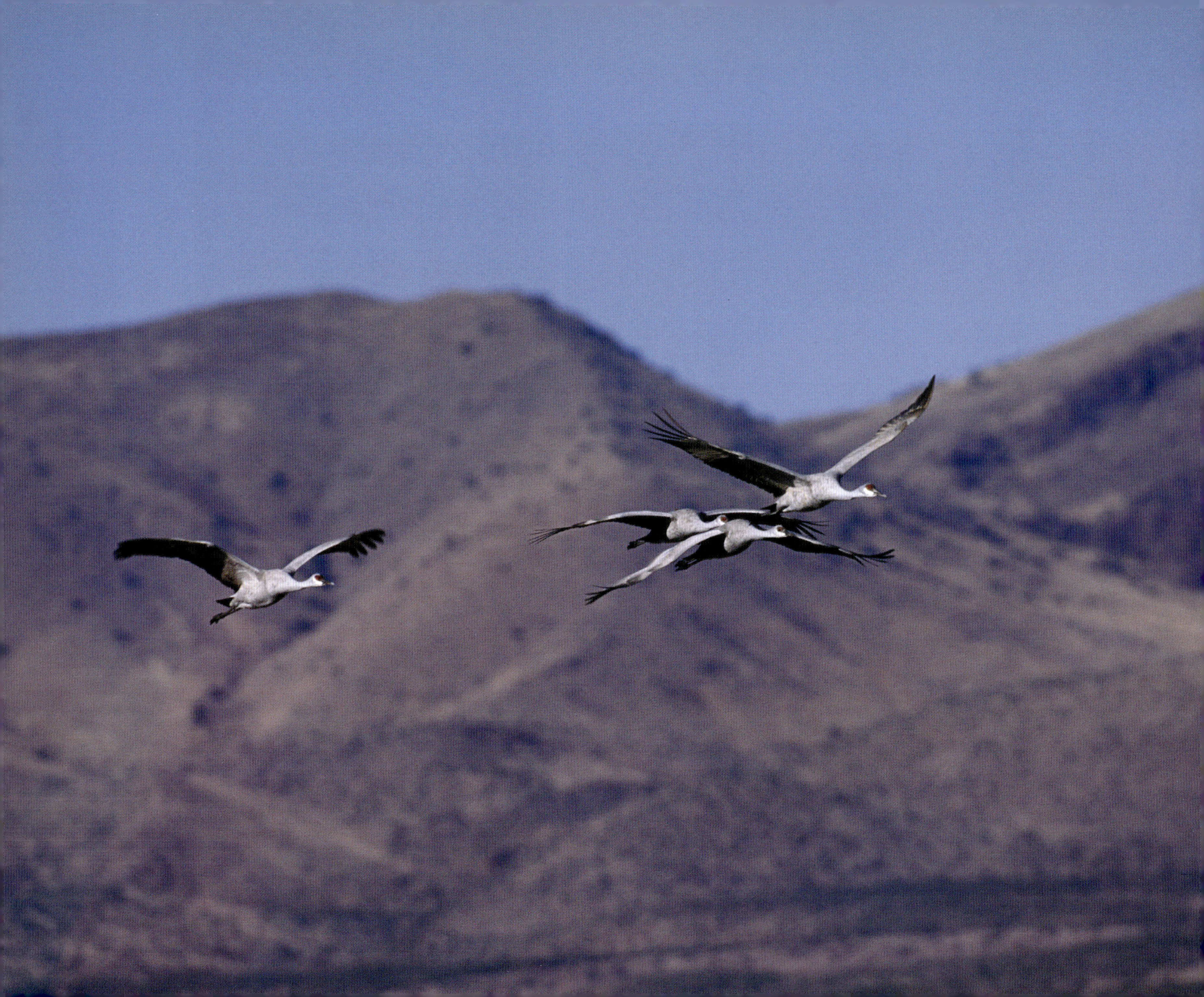

Left: Small groups of Sandhill Cranes are in constant flight across the refuge. With the Chupadero Mountains in the background, hundreds of small groups can be seen off in the distance.

Right: Irrigation channels, the heart of supplying water to the marsh systems, are often frequented by Great Blue Herons. Sometimes roosting late into the morning and even midday, the herons scan the waterways for small fish.

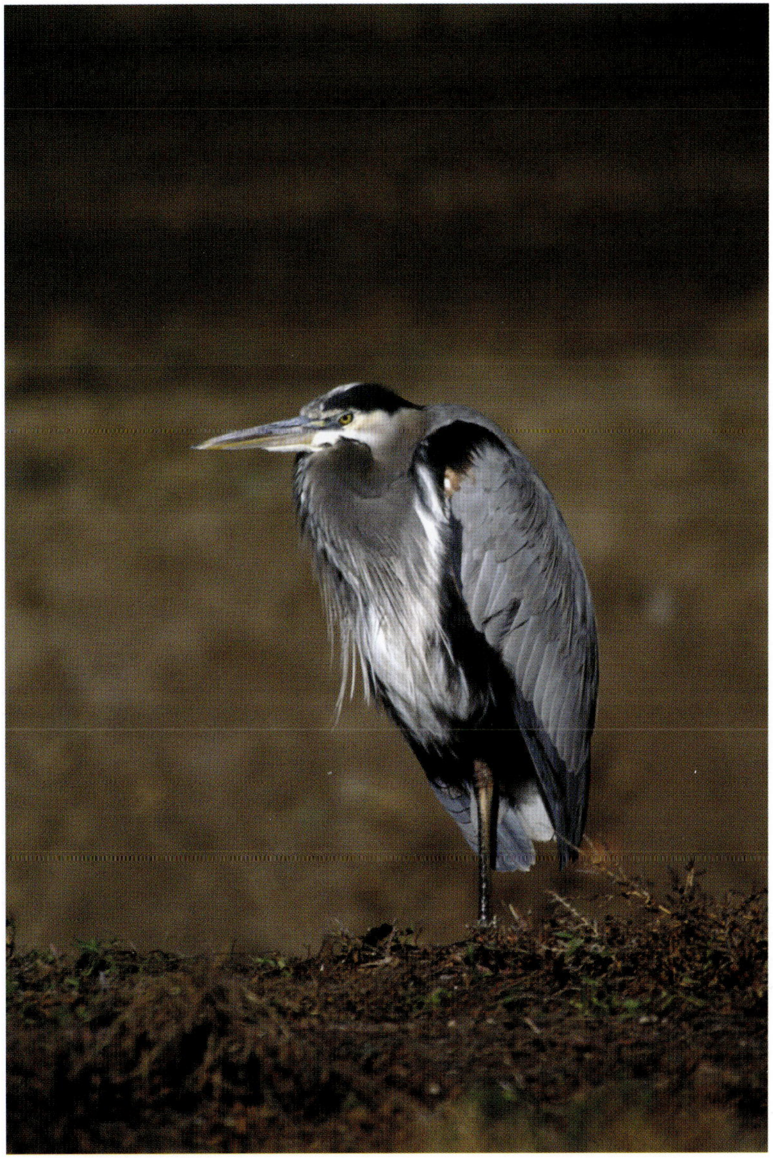

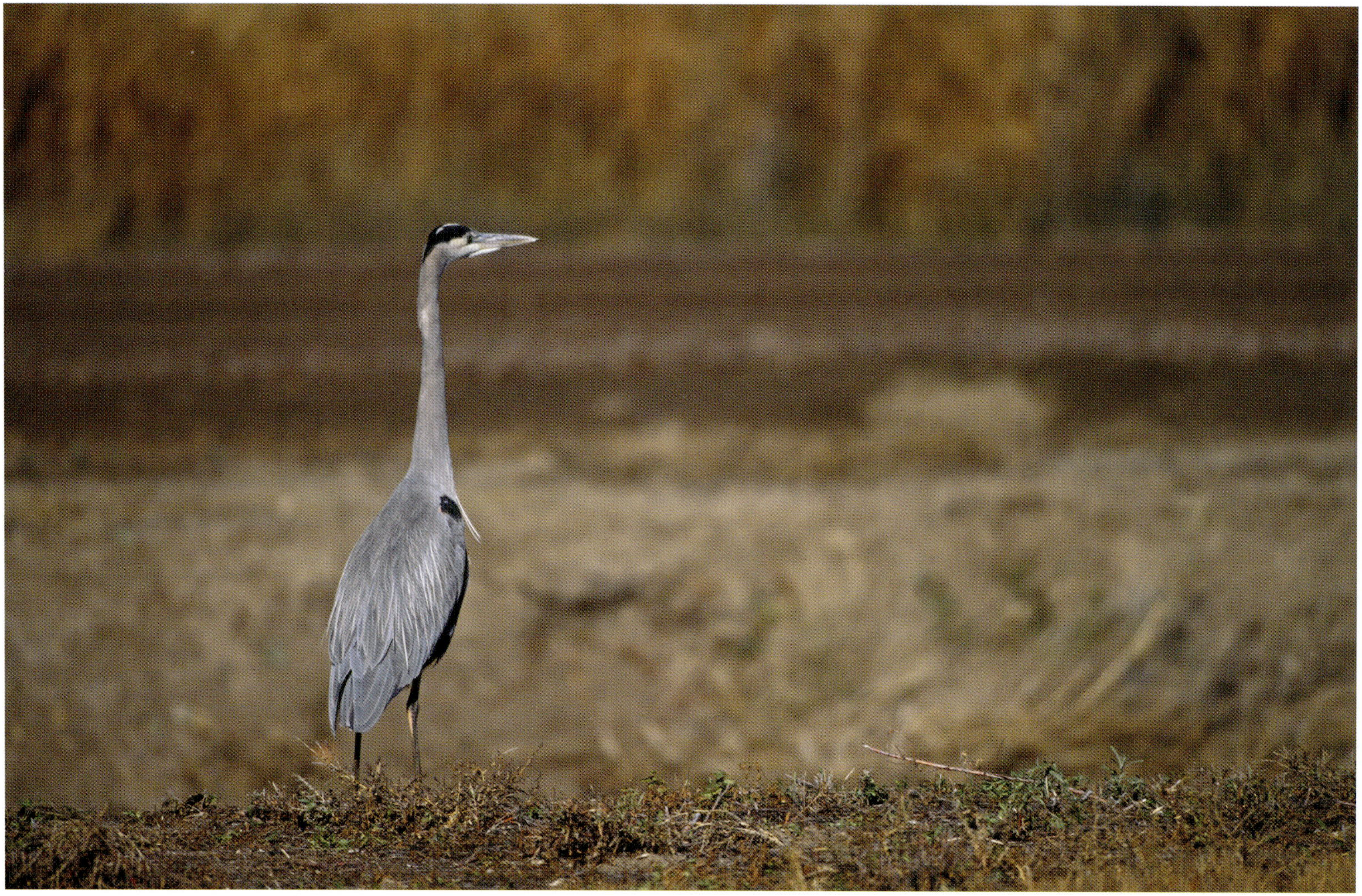

Above: When trouble or opportunities arise, herons can conveniently extend their neck to improve the viewing perspective.

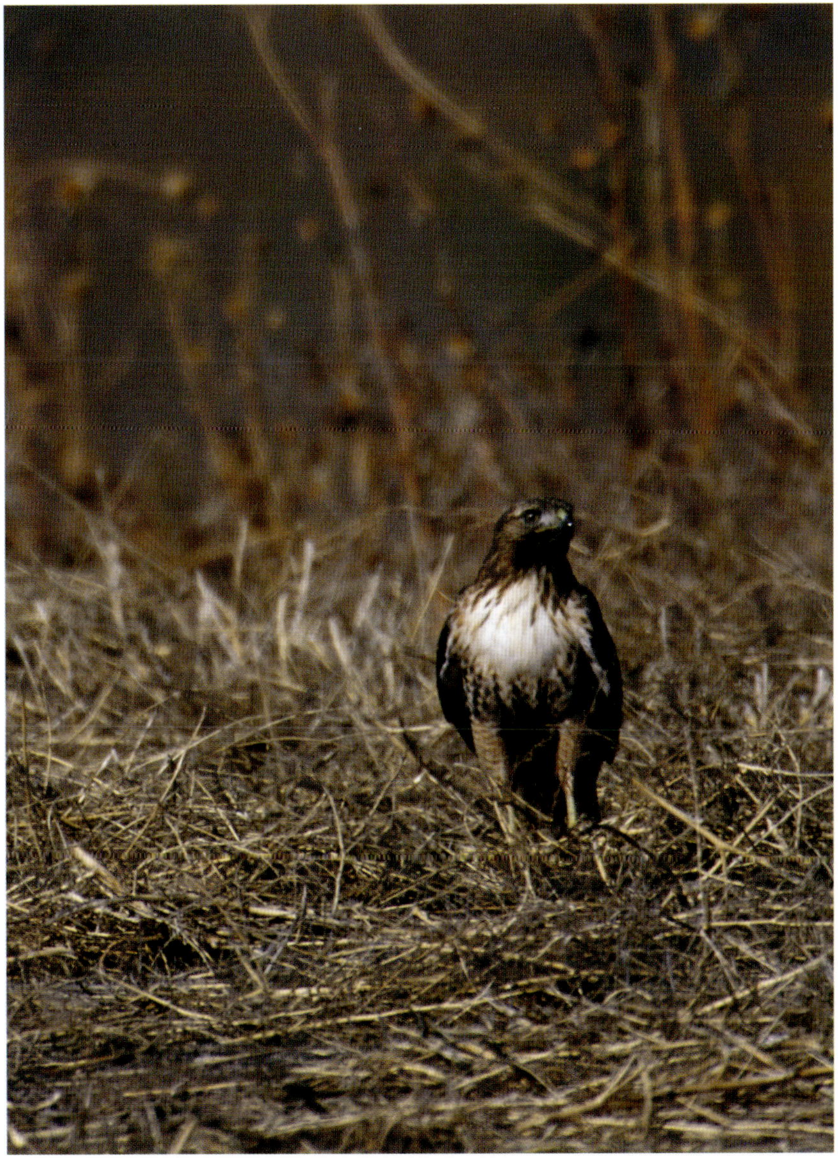

Left: Nailed. A small field mouse is under the grips of this Red-tailed Hawk. Occasionally sharing with another hawk nearby, this bird quickly finishes the meal on the ground and then bolts.

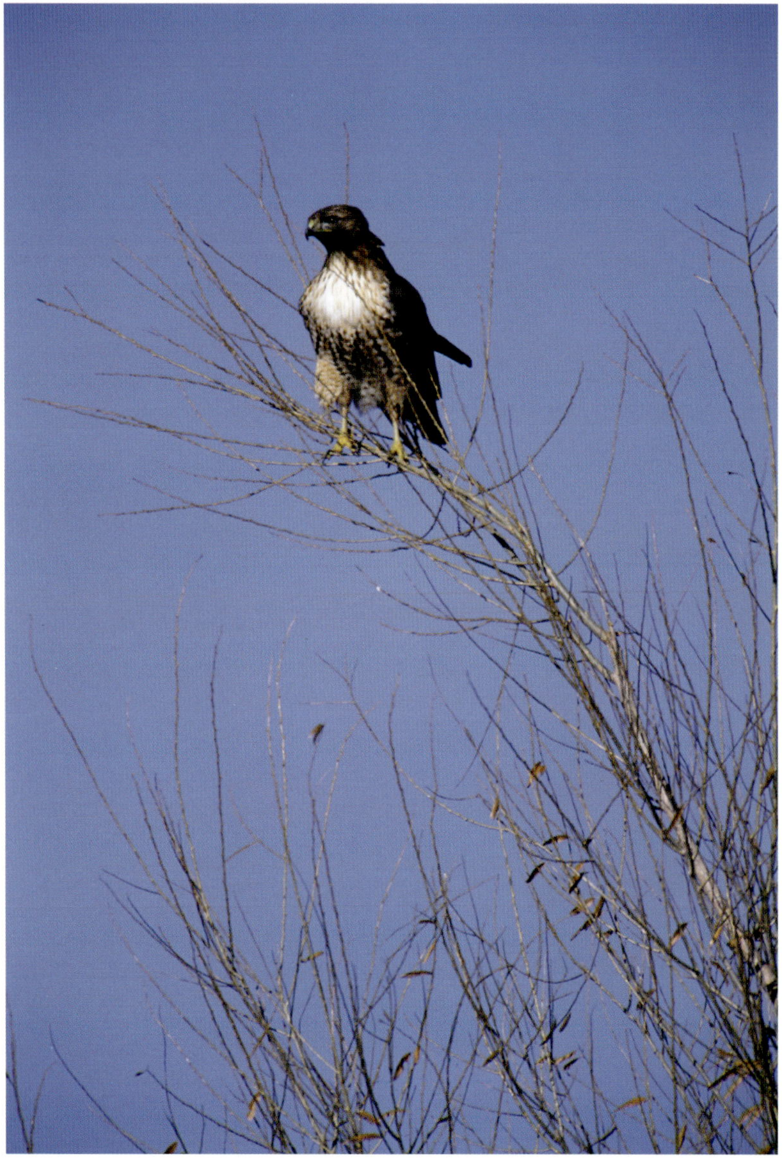

Left: Surveillance and reconnaissance are critical to the survival of raptors on the refuge. On watch, they monitor opportunities on the ground.

Right: Perched off the auto route, high in the trees, several hawks take up a vigilant watch.

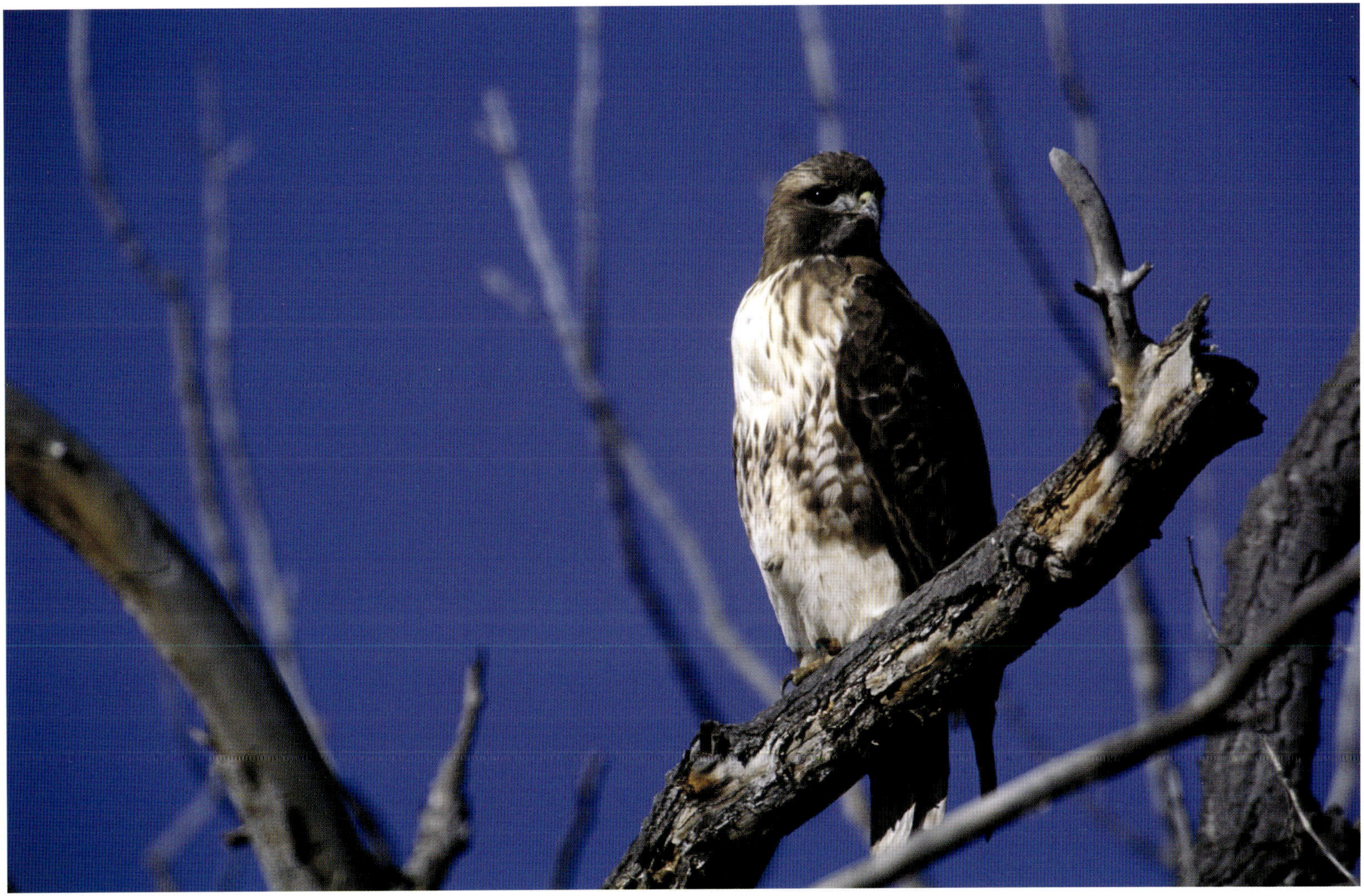

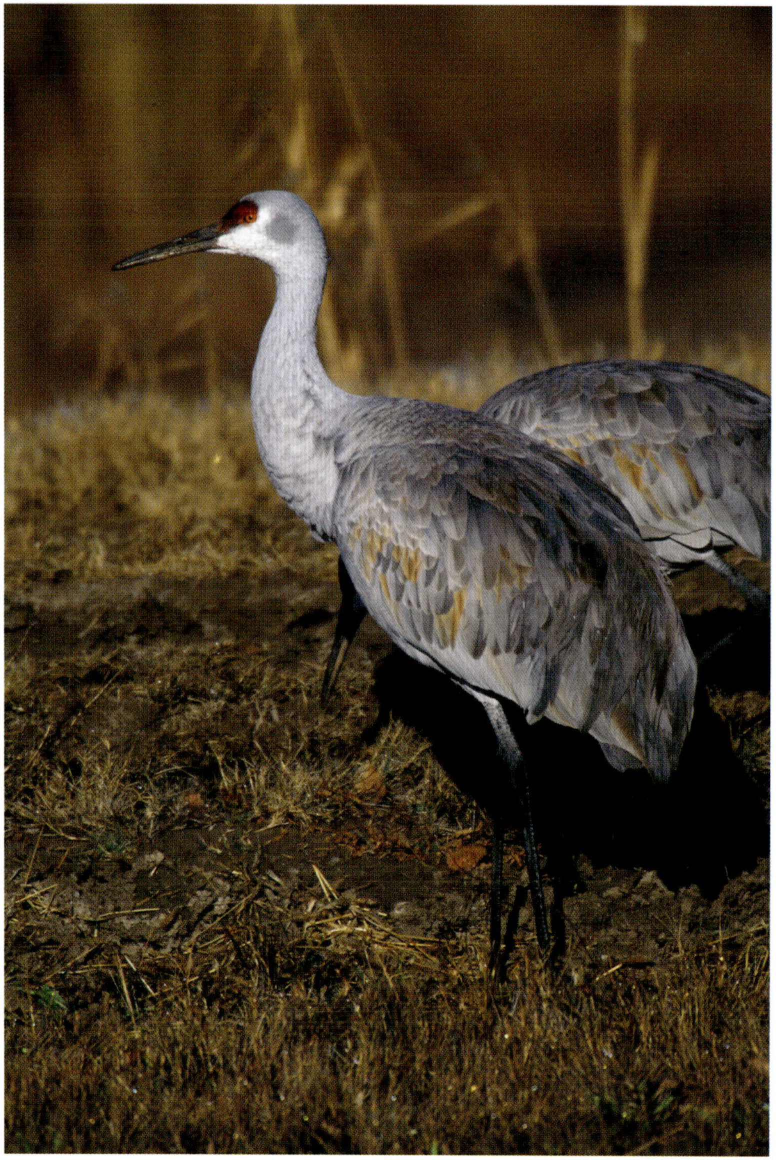

Left: As midday approaches, cranes work the fields and irrigation channels for food.

Right: While in constant view of the ground below, this hawk is locked-on to potential prey.

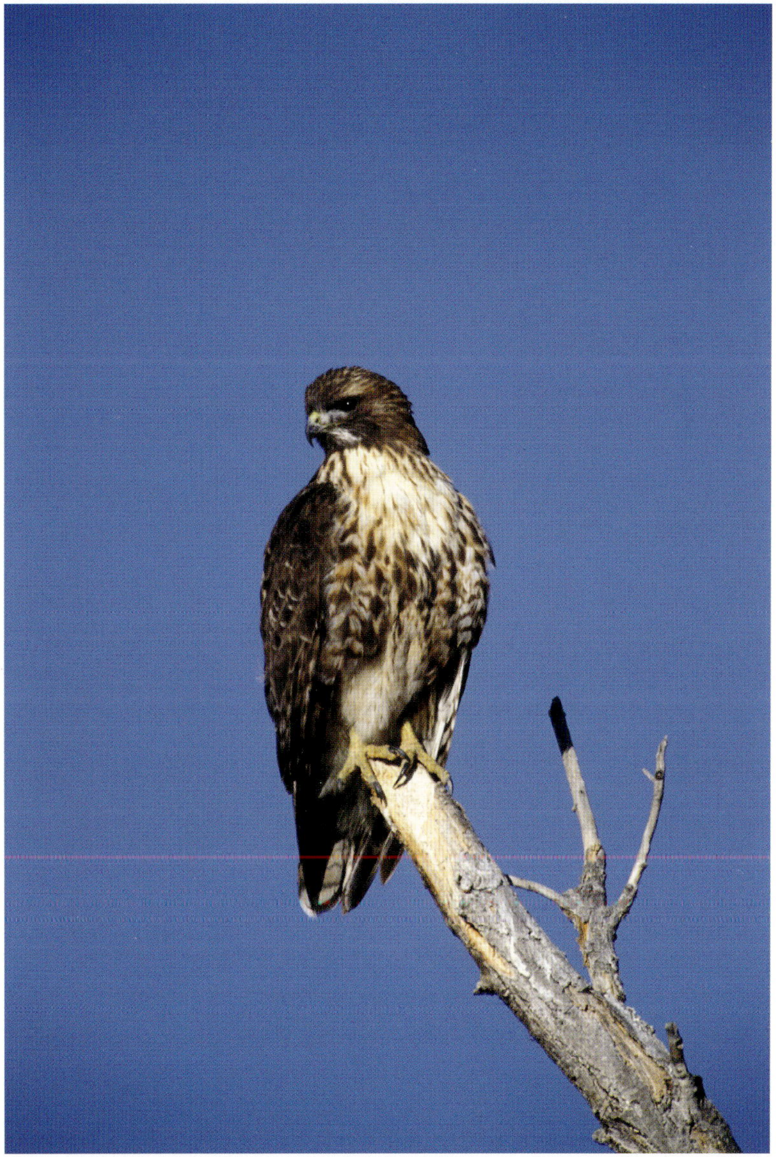

Right: Trouble. Snow Geese have been spooked into midday flight over the farm fields.

Below: Likely the work of a North Harrier or coyote, the flock can be easily spooked at a moments notice.

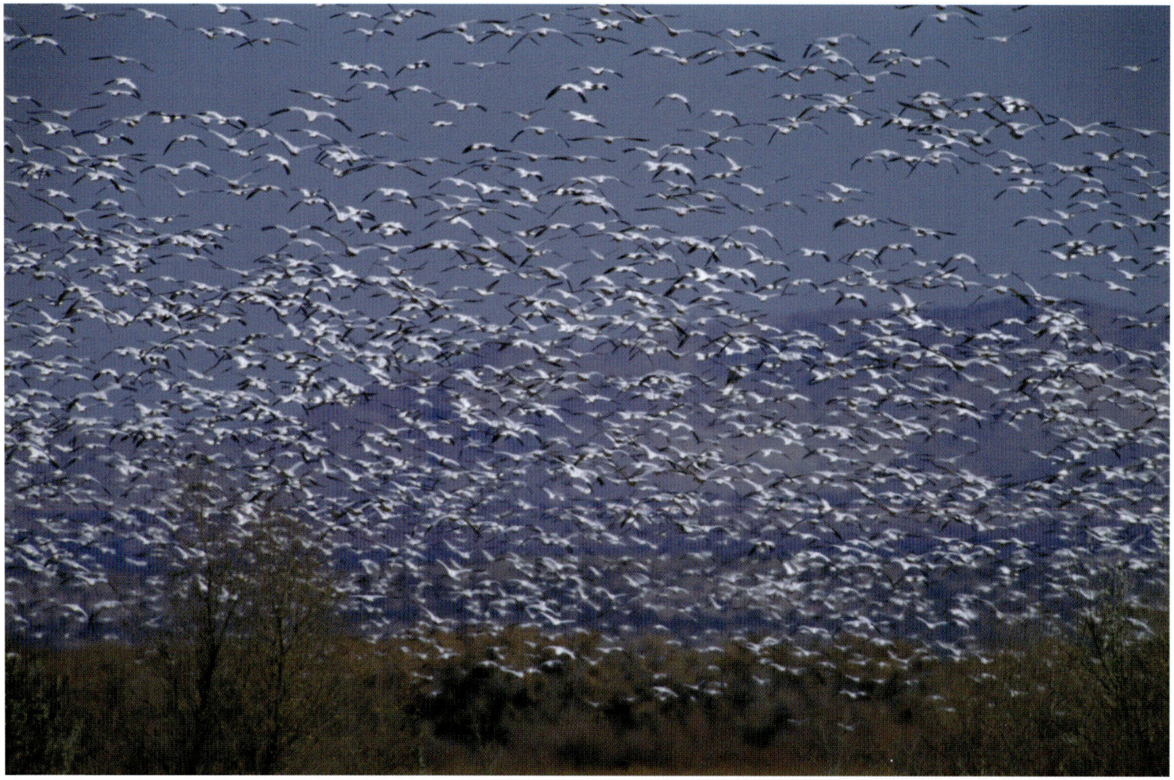

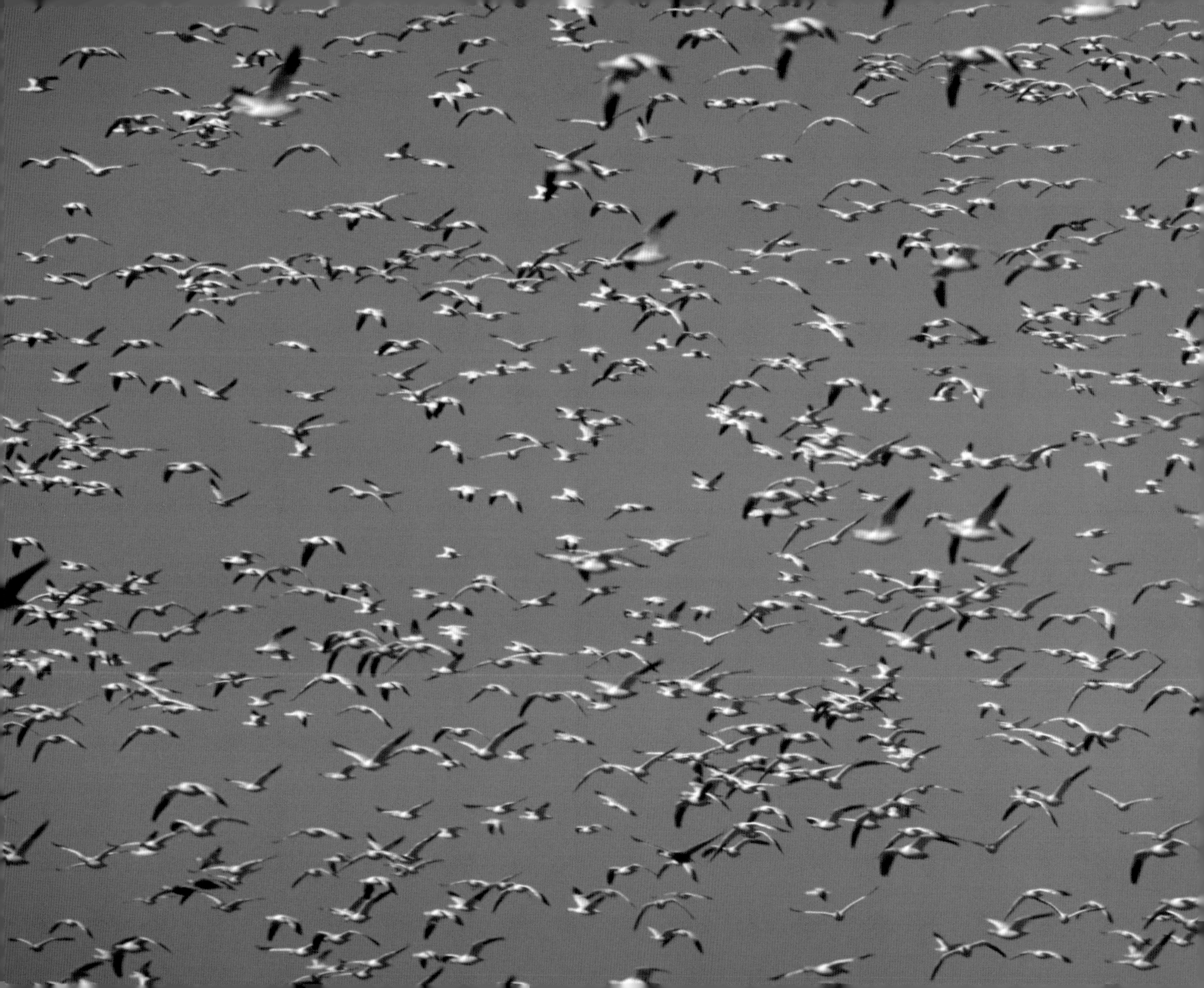

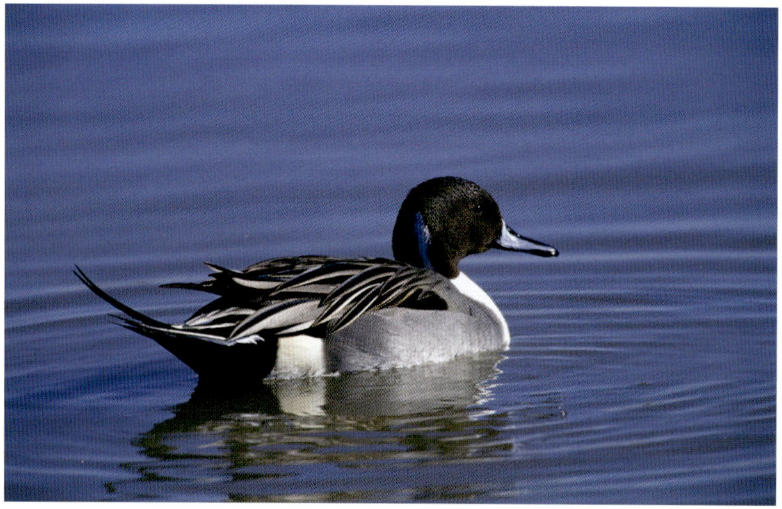

Left: A large number of Northern Pintails frequent Bosque del Apache refuge. Mid to late afternoon offers an excellent opportunity to see these birds up close.

Right: Into the air. A small flock of Snow Geese immediately gather up for a short flight around the cornfield.

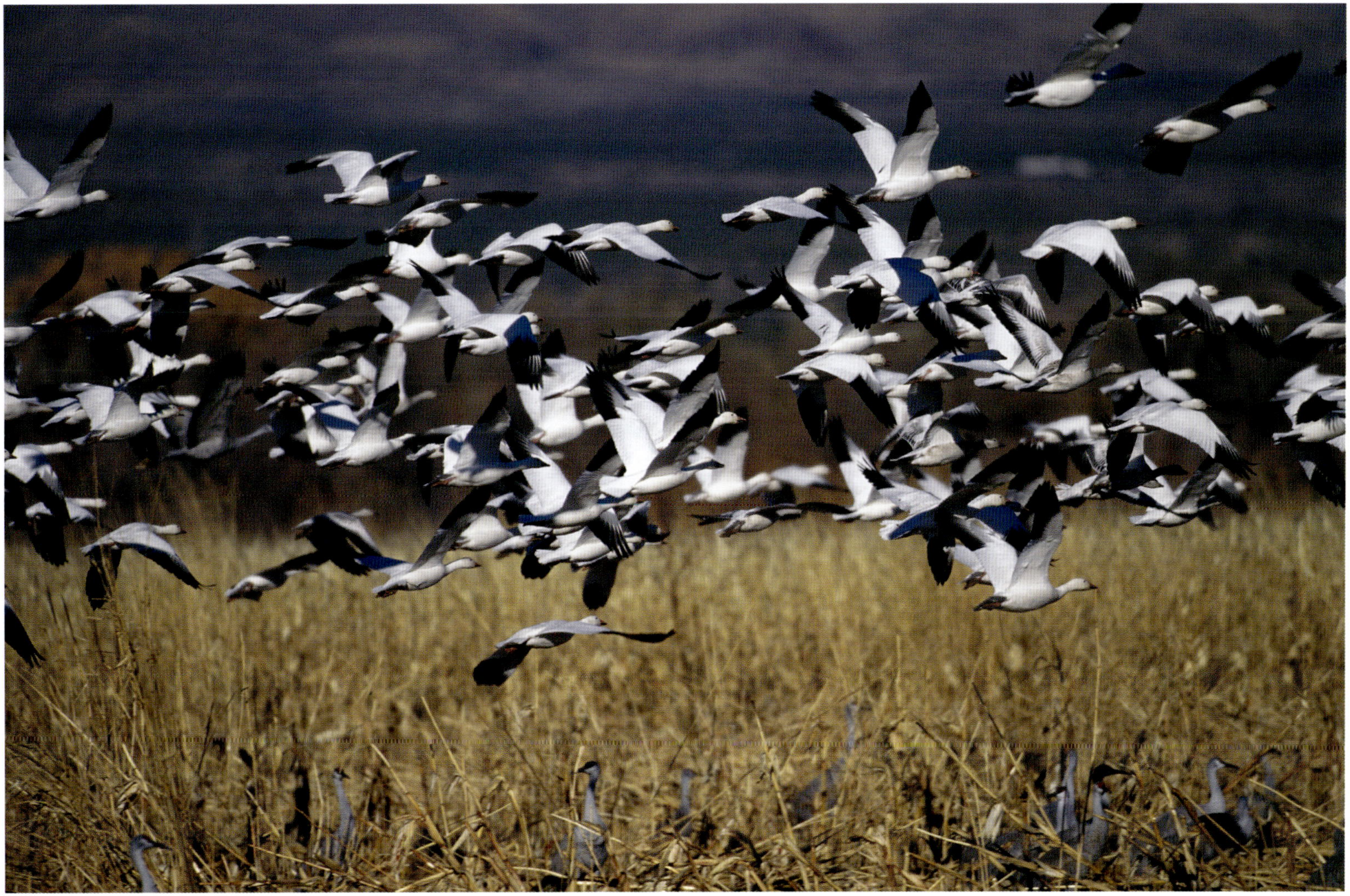

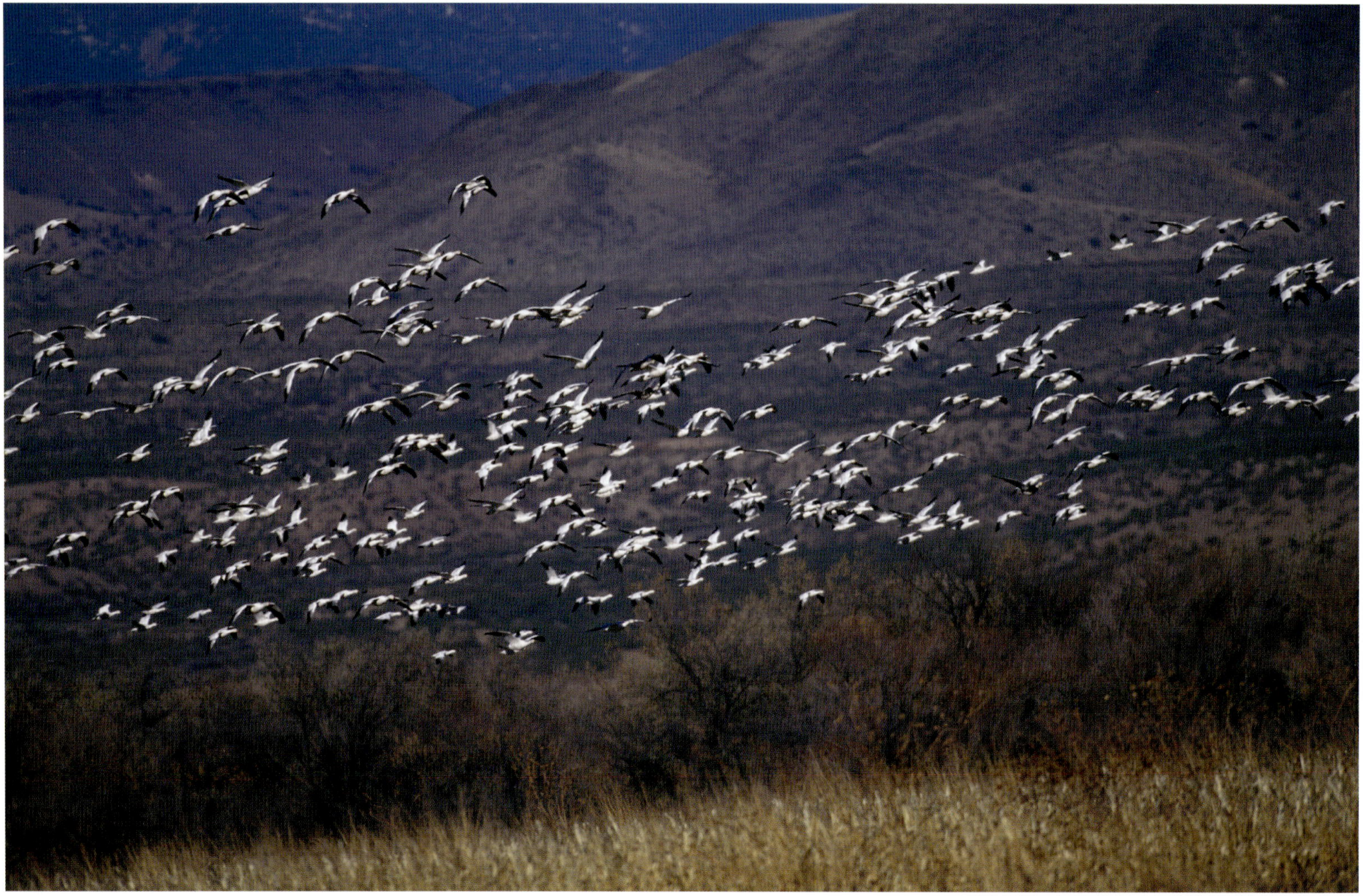

Above: Circling the field, the geese reposition to avert a pesky Northern Harrier.

Right: A Say's Phoebe is one of many perching birds found throughout the refuge.

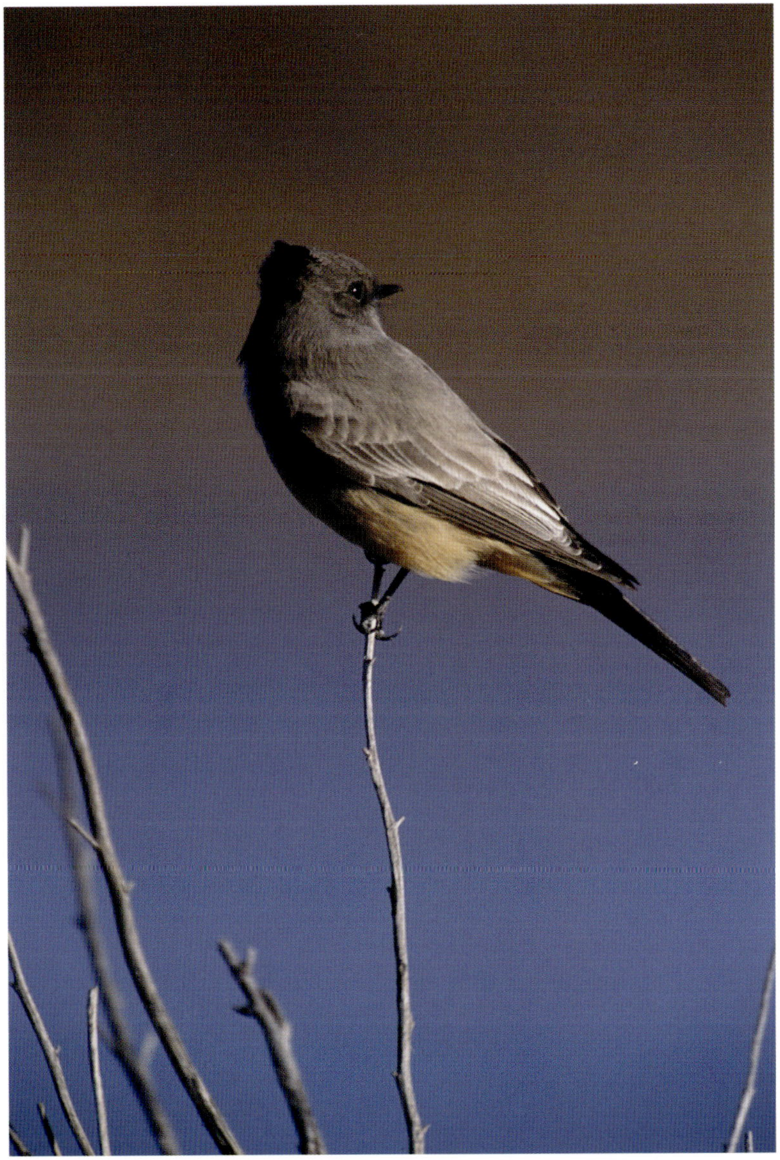

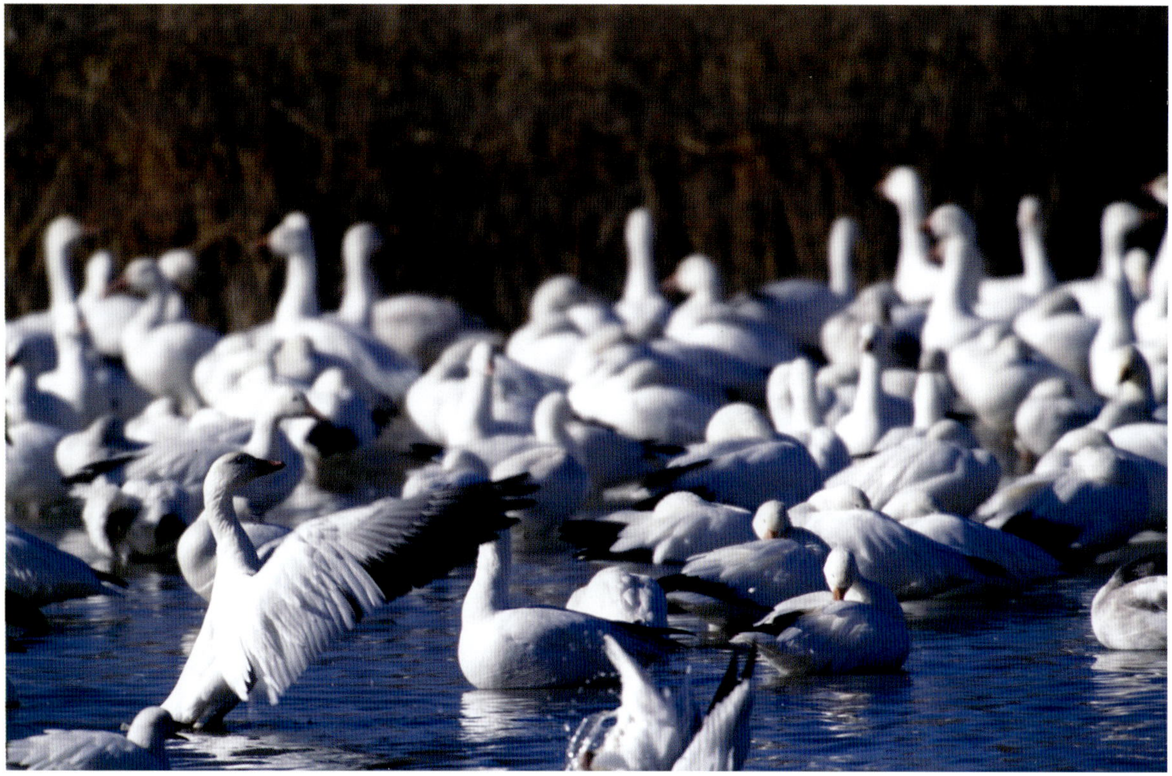

Above: As afternoon gets long in the day, Snow Geese jam a marsh observation area. Thousands take in the marsh waters while photographers and visitors alike observe covertly through the Phil Norton Observation blind.

Right: Beautiful Snow Goose resting for the evening's flight.

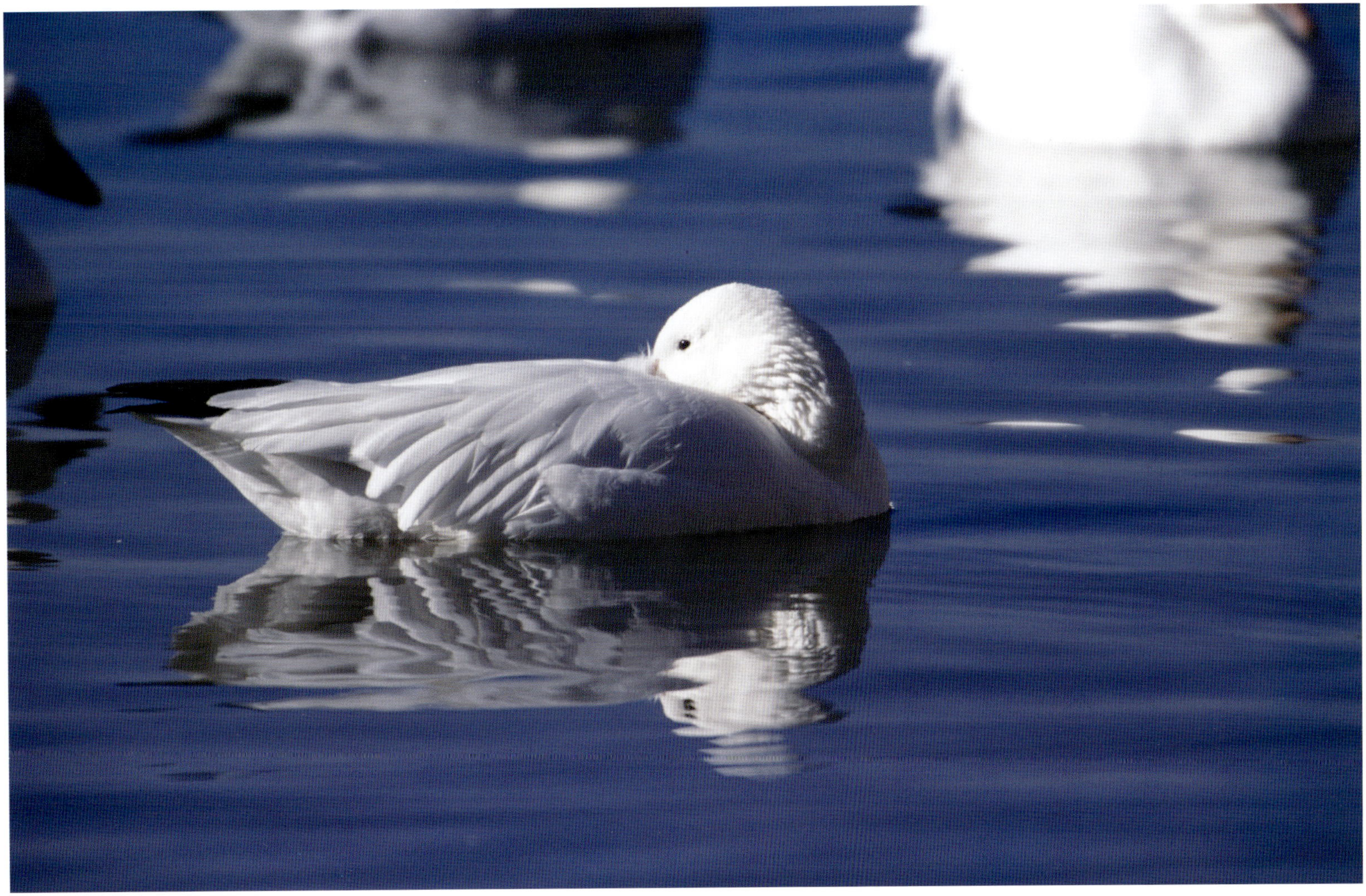

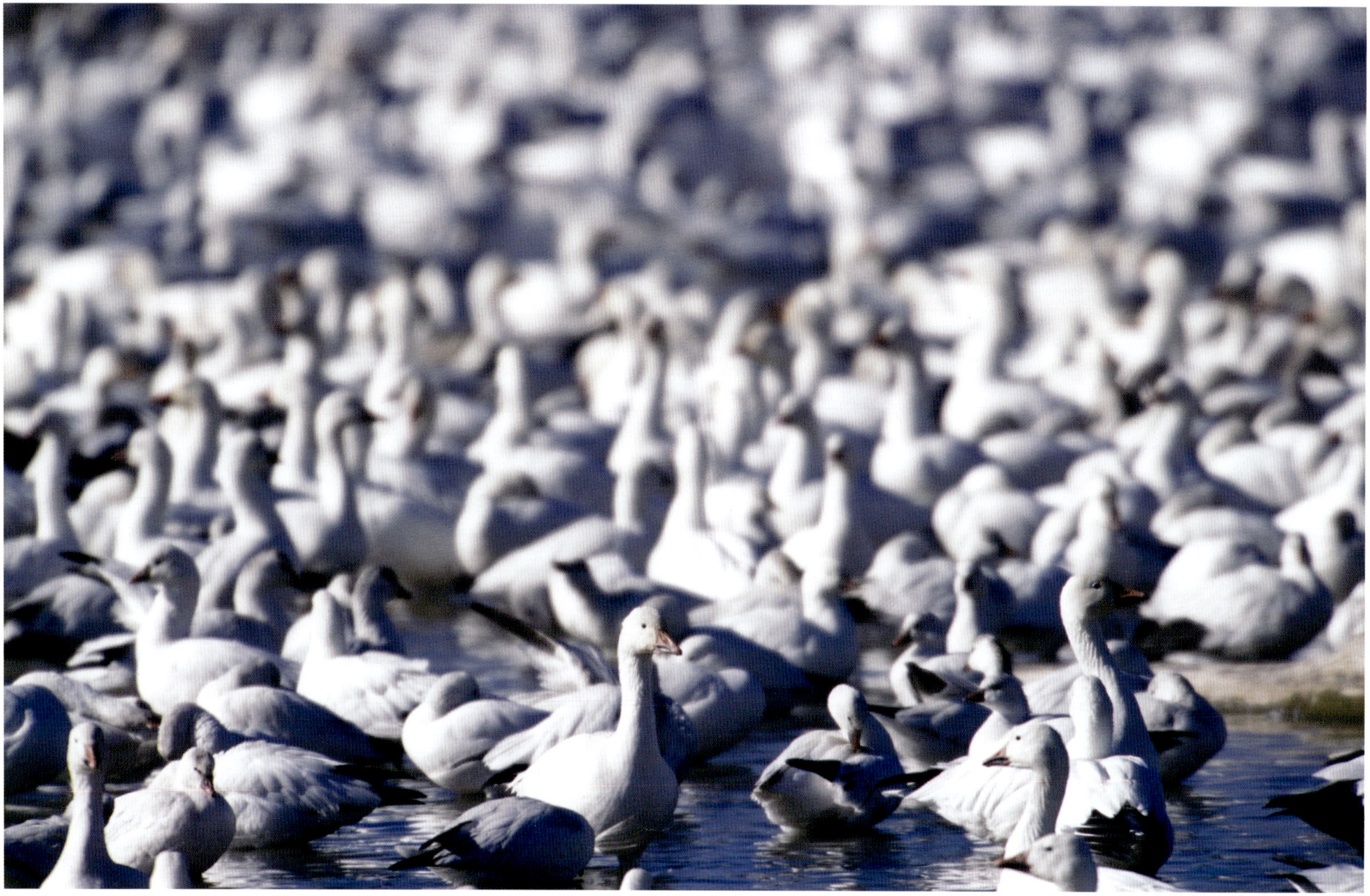

Above: A loud chatter carries on between the Snow Geese. Thousands float along while others are on constant watch for intruders.

Right: Along the auto route, an occasional Roadrunner can be seen. Magnificent plumage and eyes, this bird is ready for action.

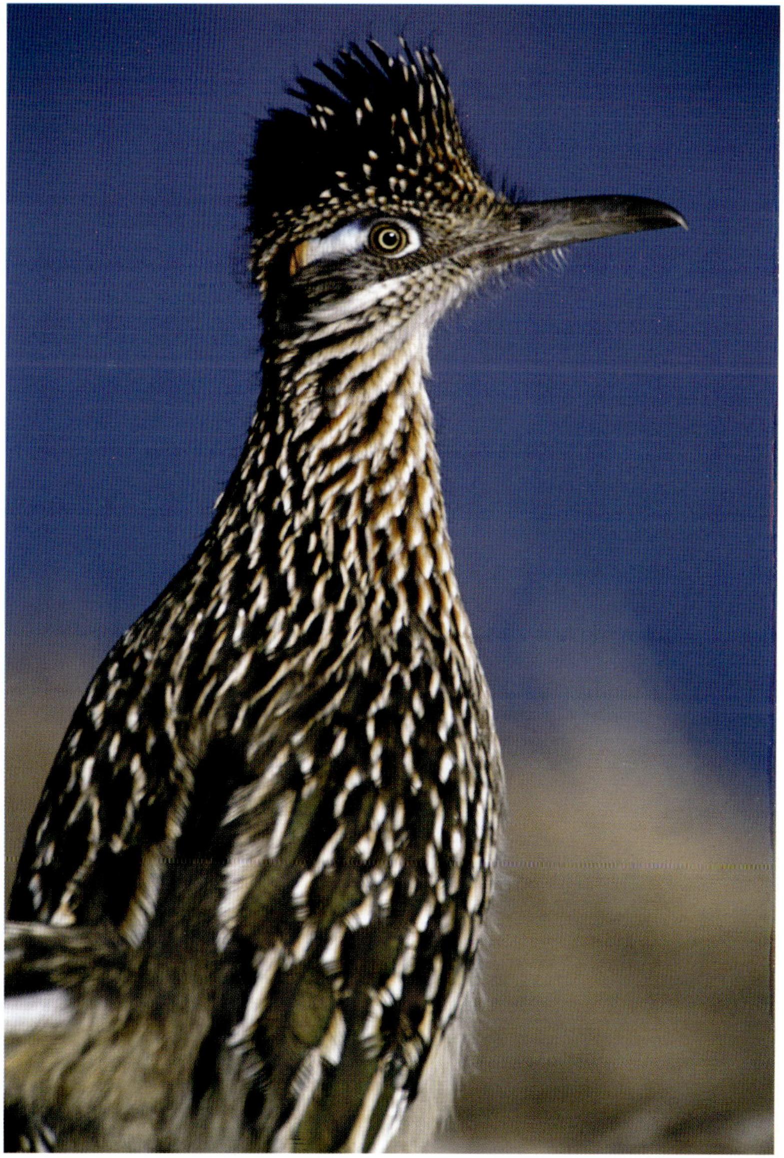

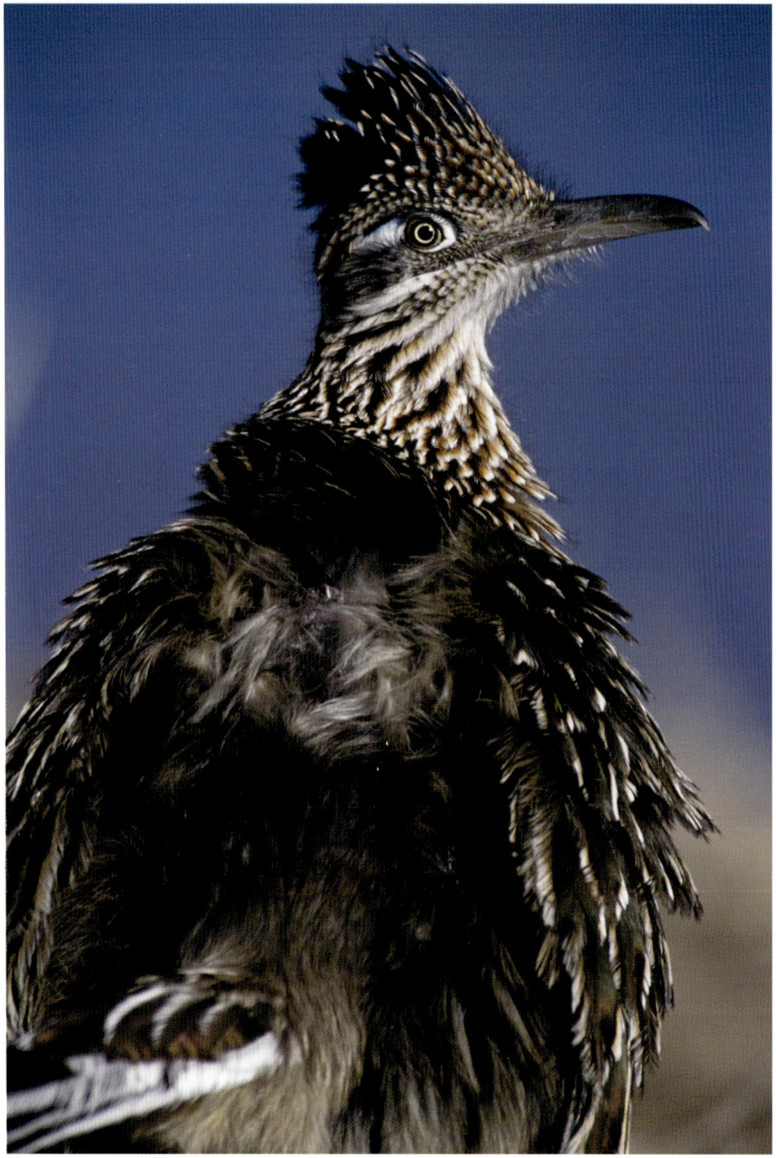

Left: Hold-on, I m bigger than you think.

Right: Throughout the year access by the public is managed to ensure sensitive areas are not disturbed at critical times of migration. This juvenile Red-tailed Hawk was more than willing to follow the rules.

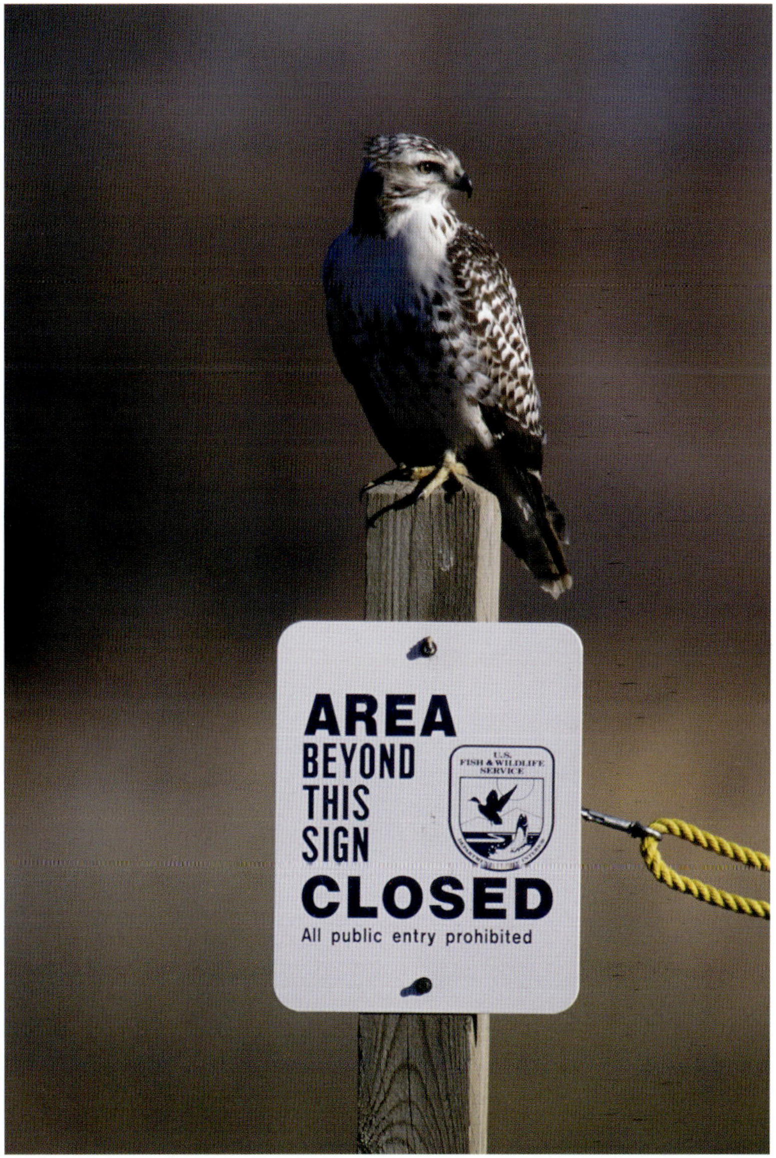
AREA
BEYOND
THIS
SIGN
CLOSED
All public entry prohibited
U.S.
FISH & WILDLIFE
SERVICE

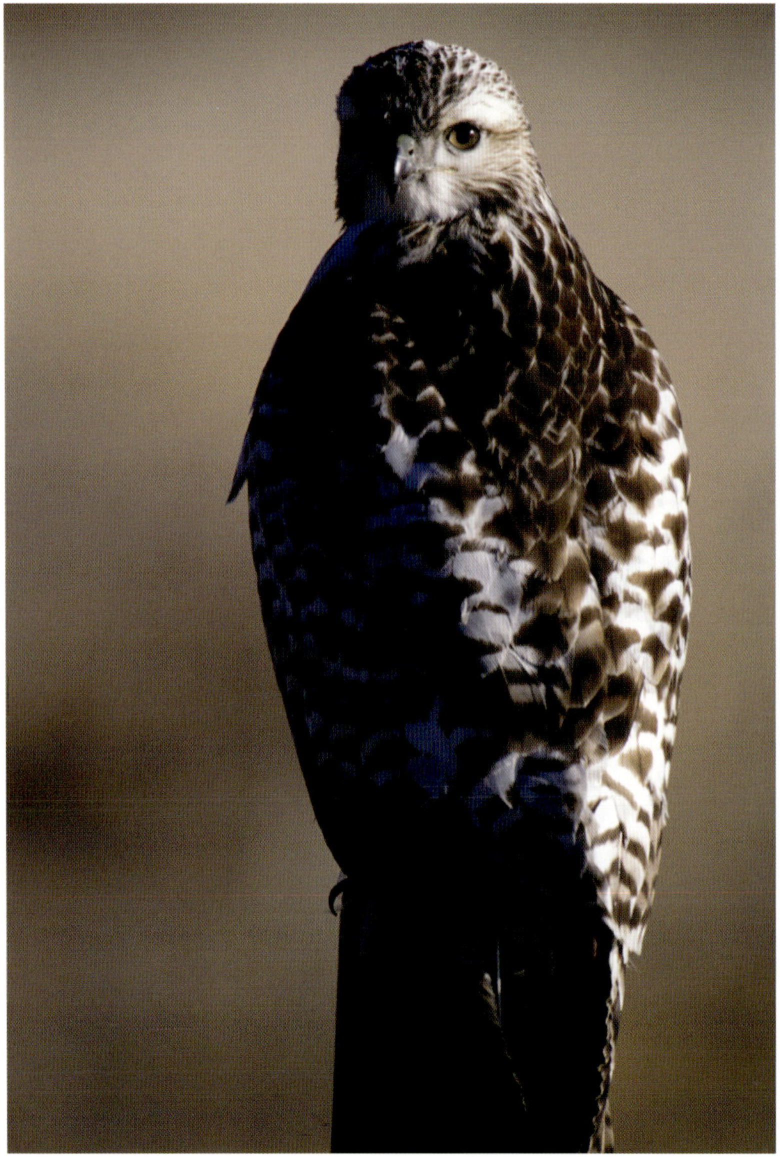

Left: With keen eyesight the Red-tailed Hawk is on the watch for prey and photographers.

Right: With the sun setting, the red-tail sizes up an opportunity.

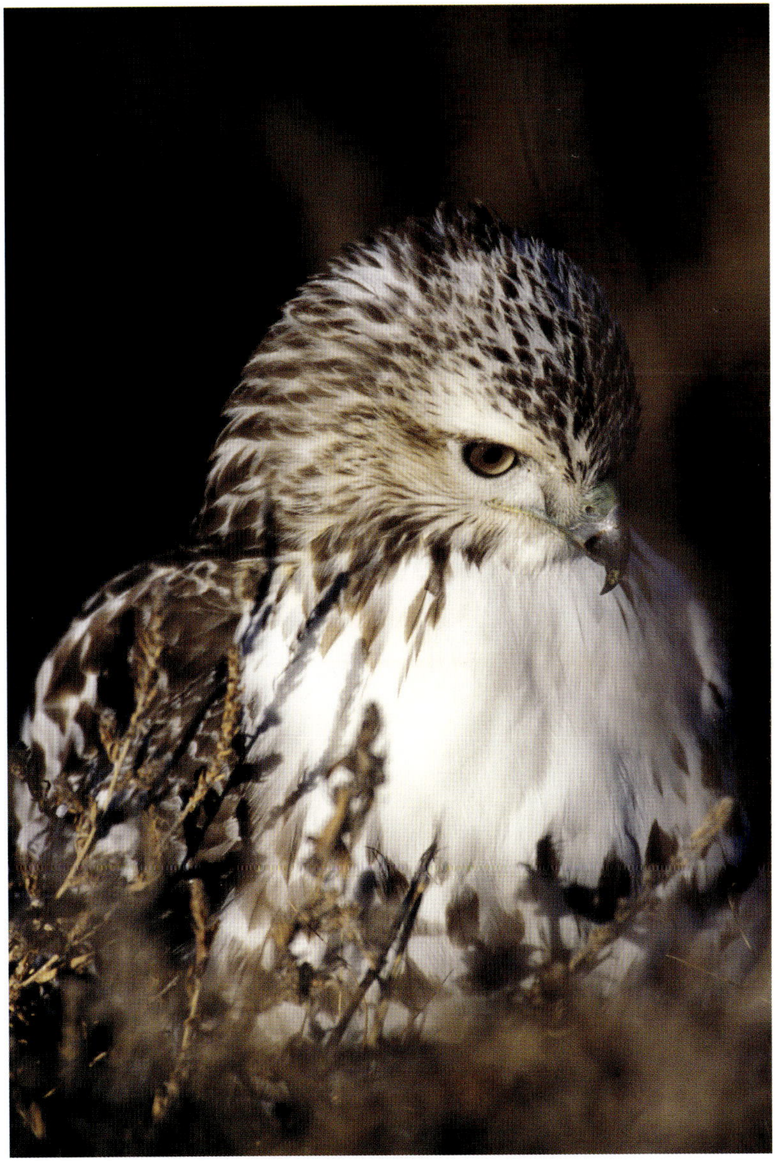

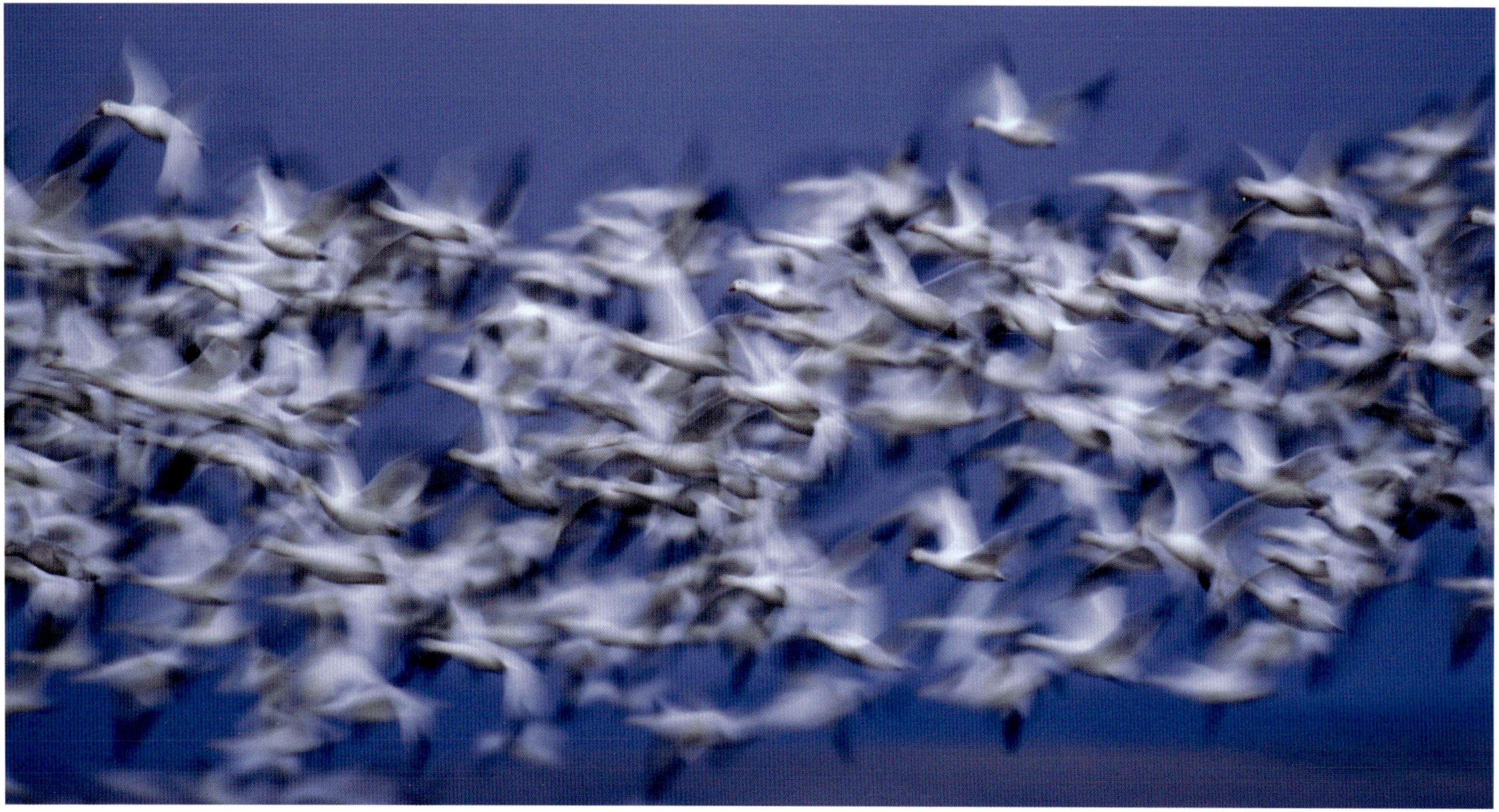

Above: As the light quickly fades, a blizzard of Snow Geese take the final flight of the evening.

Right: Once again, the rhythm of the day slows. Time for the Sandhill Crane to take on water and settle in for the night.

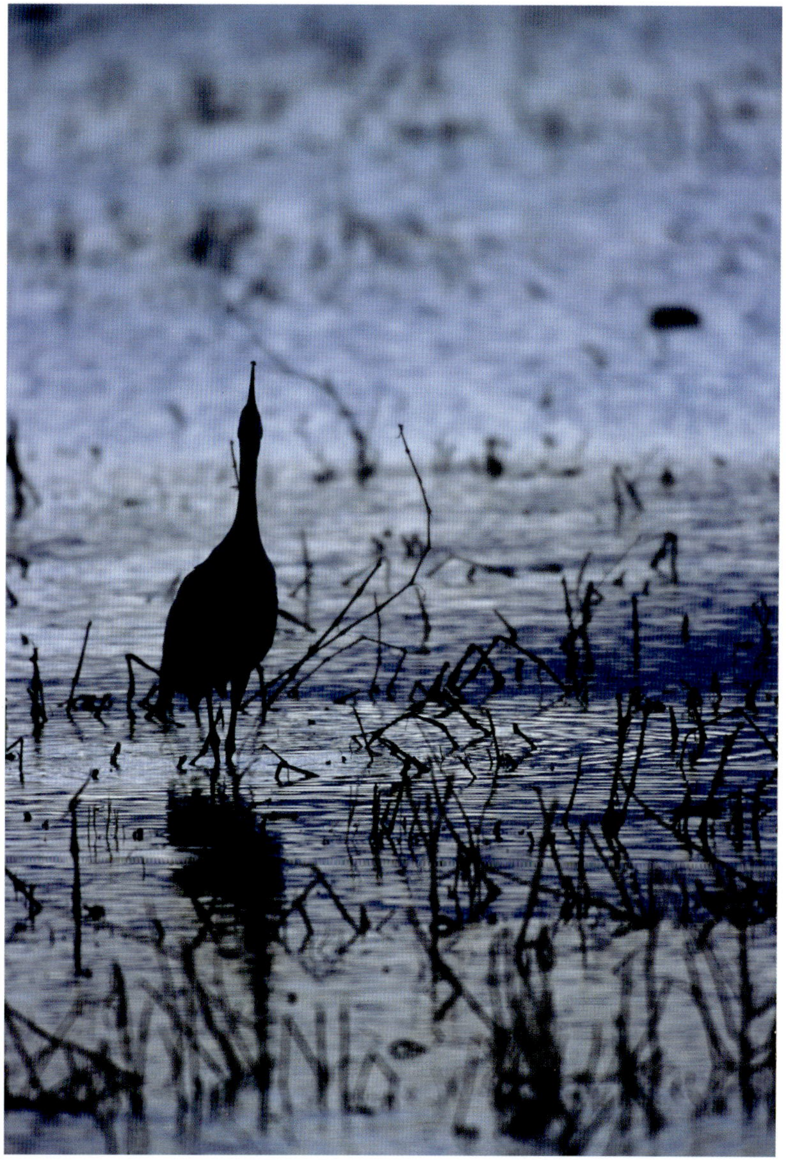

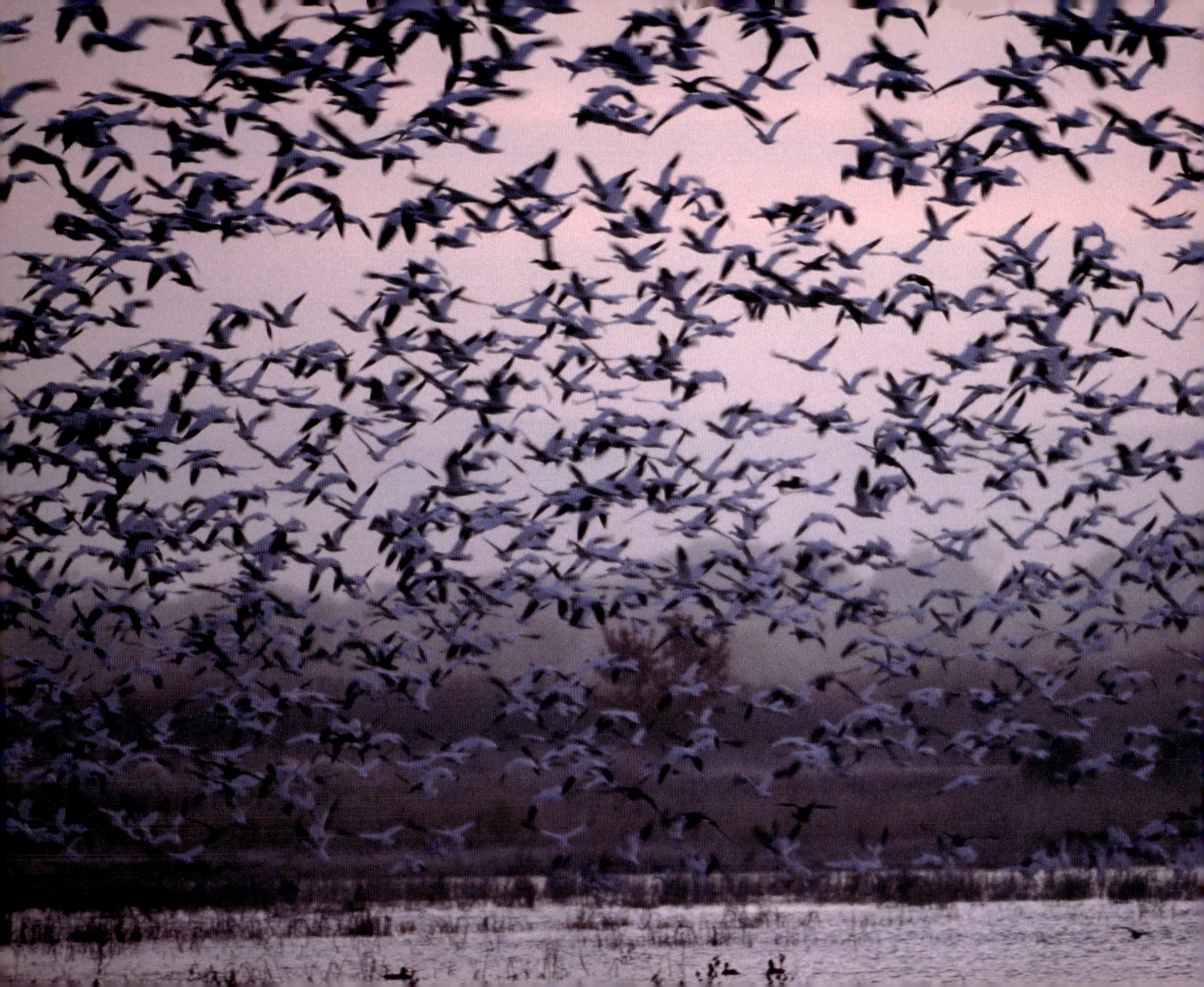

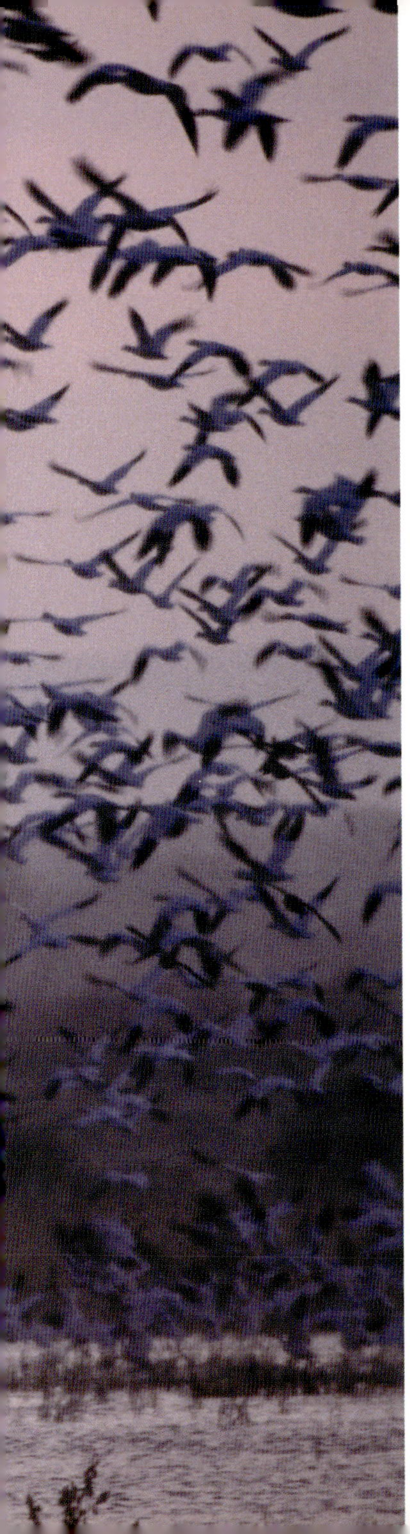

Left: Daybreak. From the Flight Deck observation platform, thousands of Snow Geese erupt in an explosion of color and noise. The rhythm of life on the refuge is renewed.

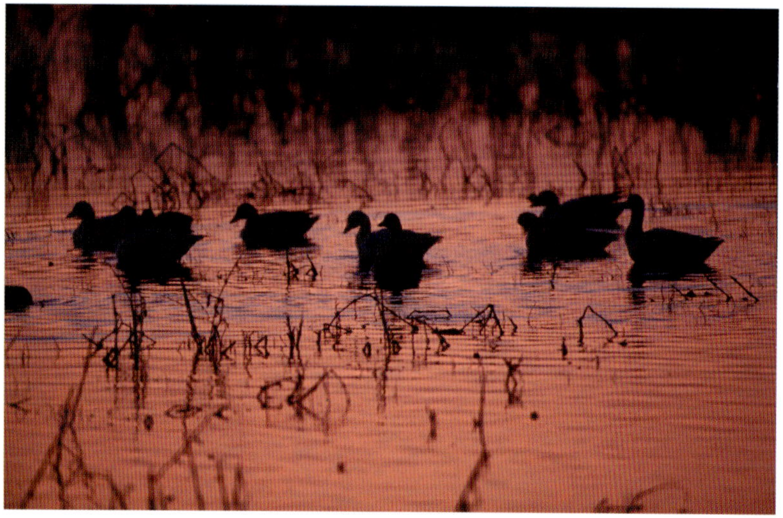

Left: Against a red background of the New Mexico sky, a small flock of geese observe the morning fly-out.

Right: With the sun up, flocks of Snow Geese take to flight again.

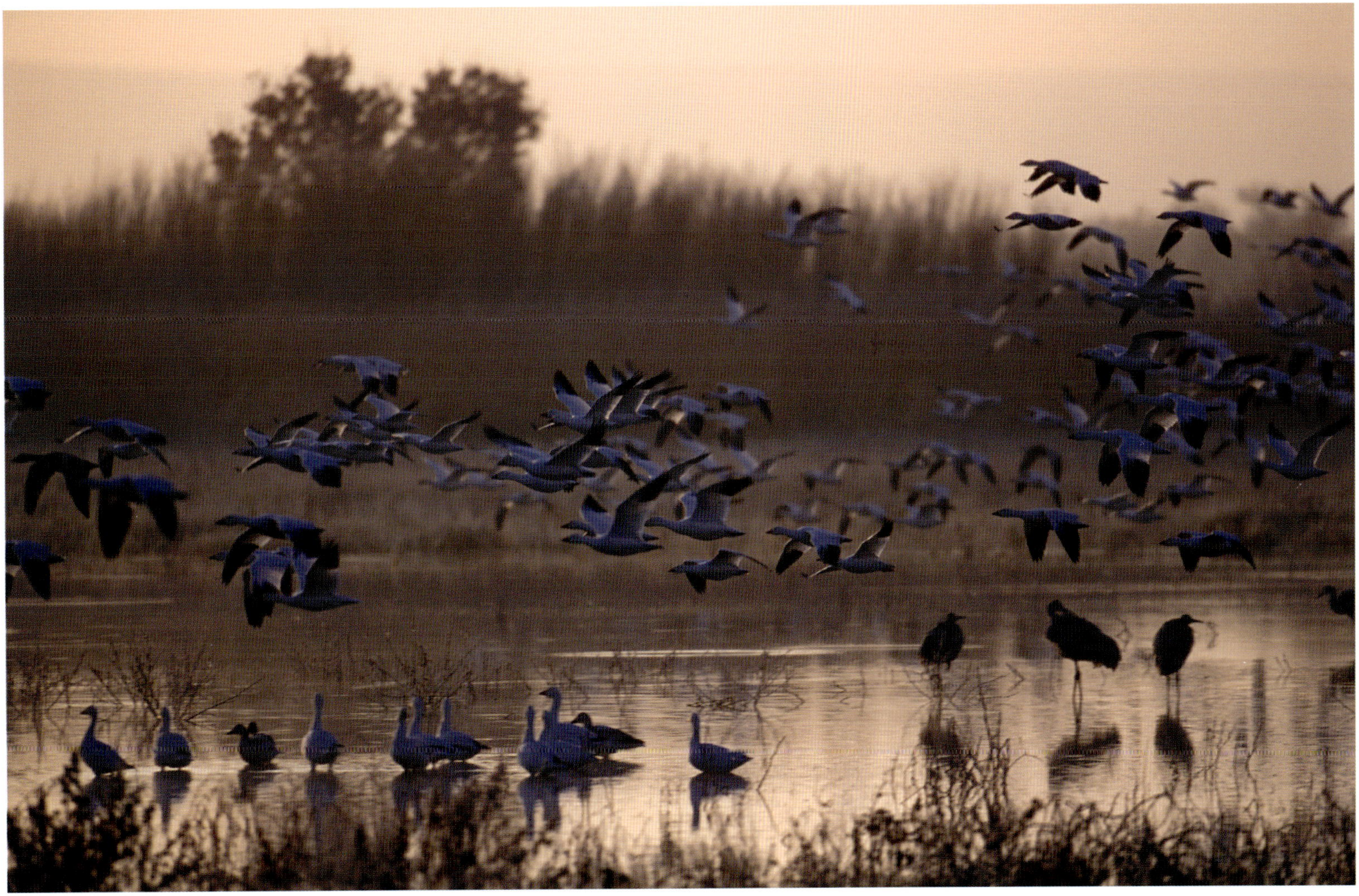

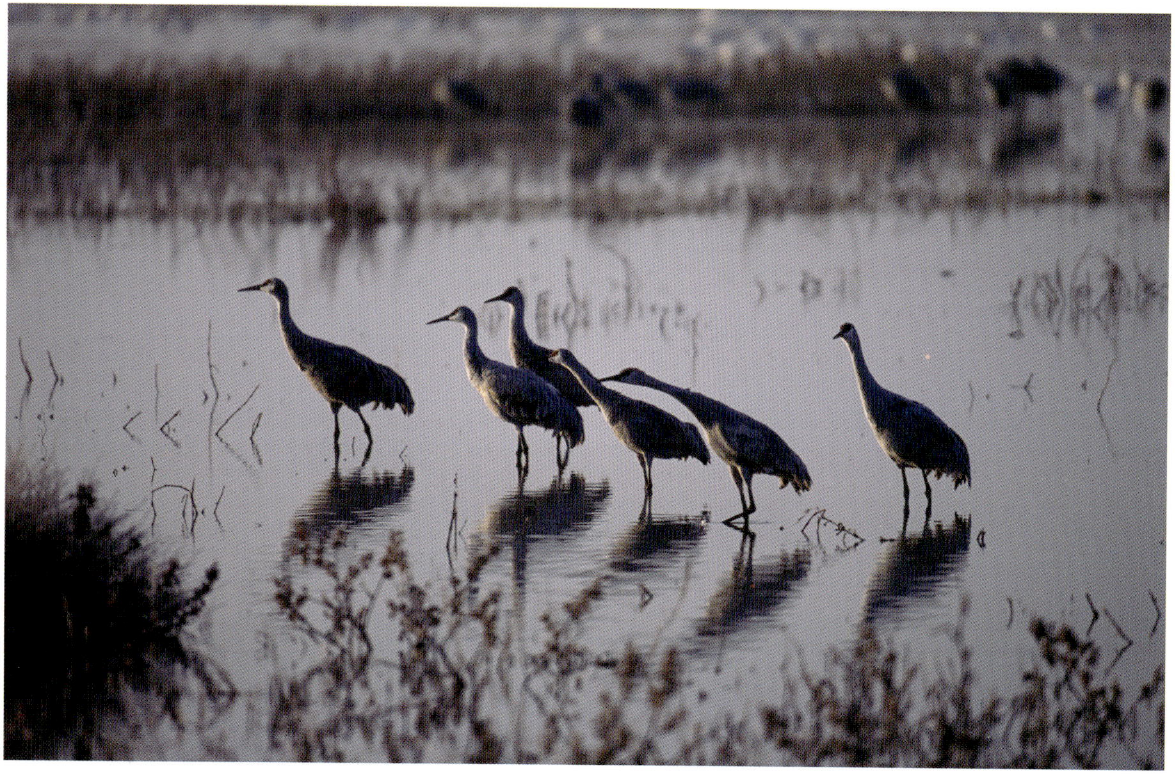

Above: Just as the prior day, several cranes marshal for position in preparation for flight at the Flight Deck.

Right: With wings spread and a swift run, the cranes take-off.

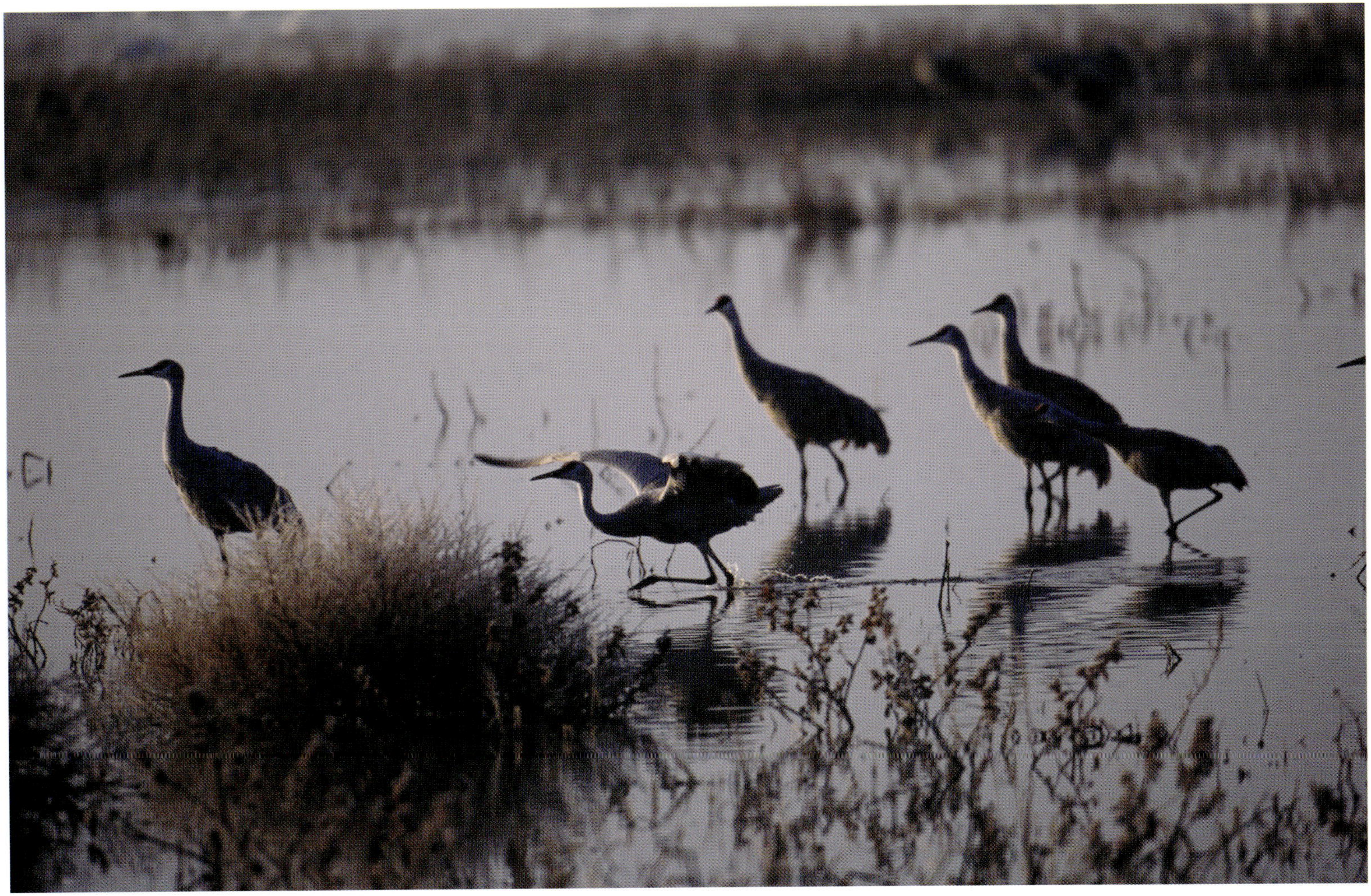

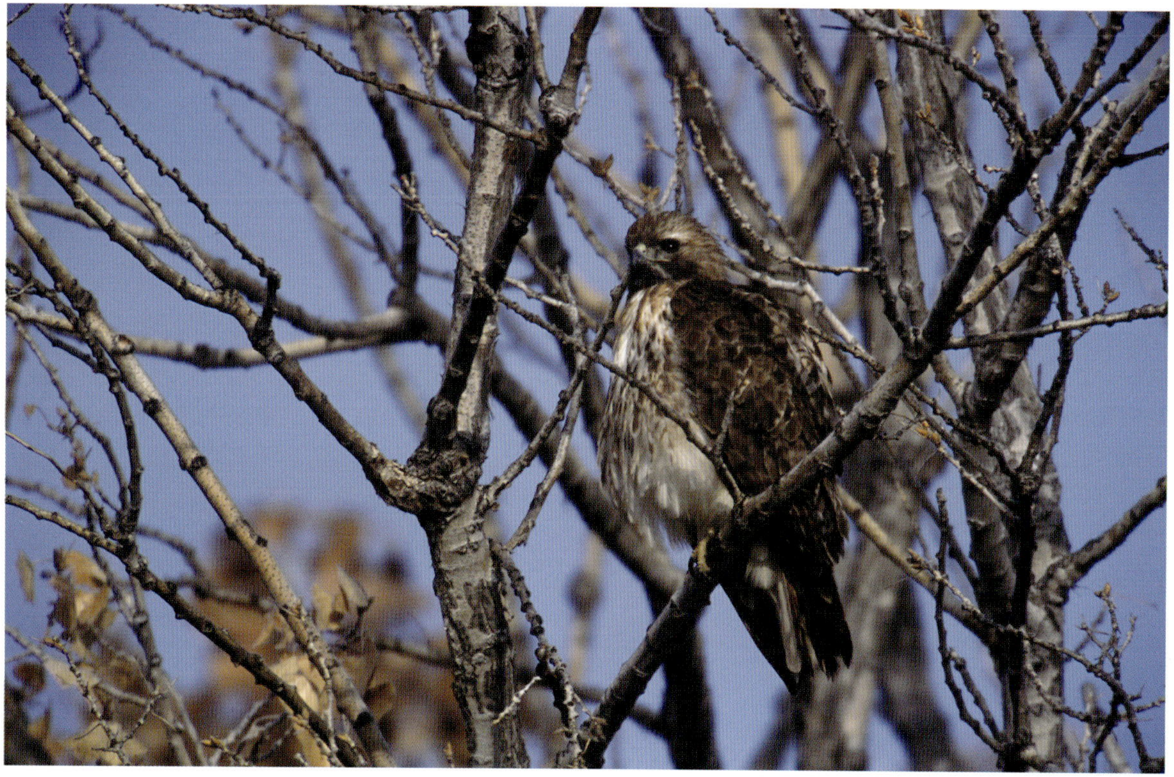

Above: Returning from the prior day, this hawk has taken up surveillance of the marsh from the same location.

Right: Nested in the tamarisk, also known as salt cedar, the Snowy Egrets roost close together in the same pond.

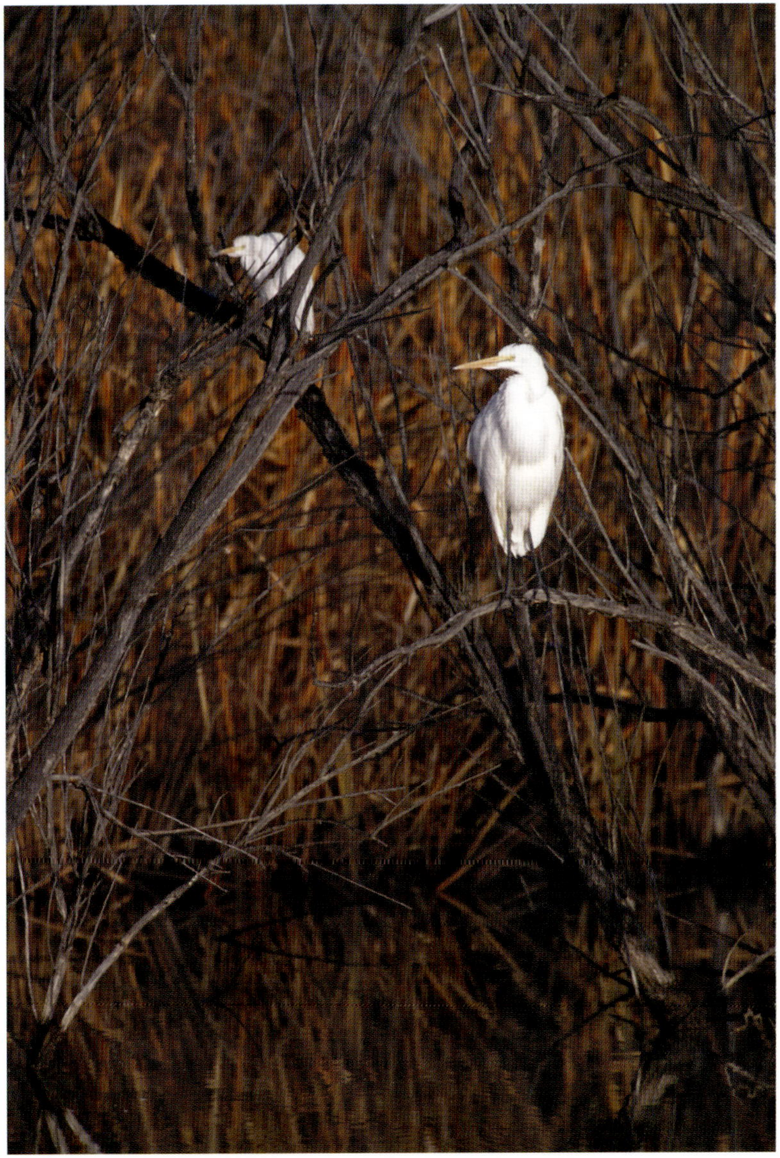

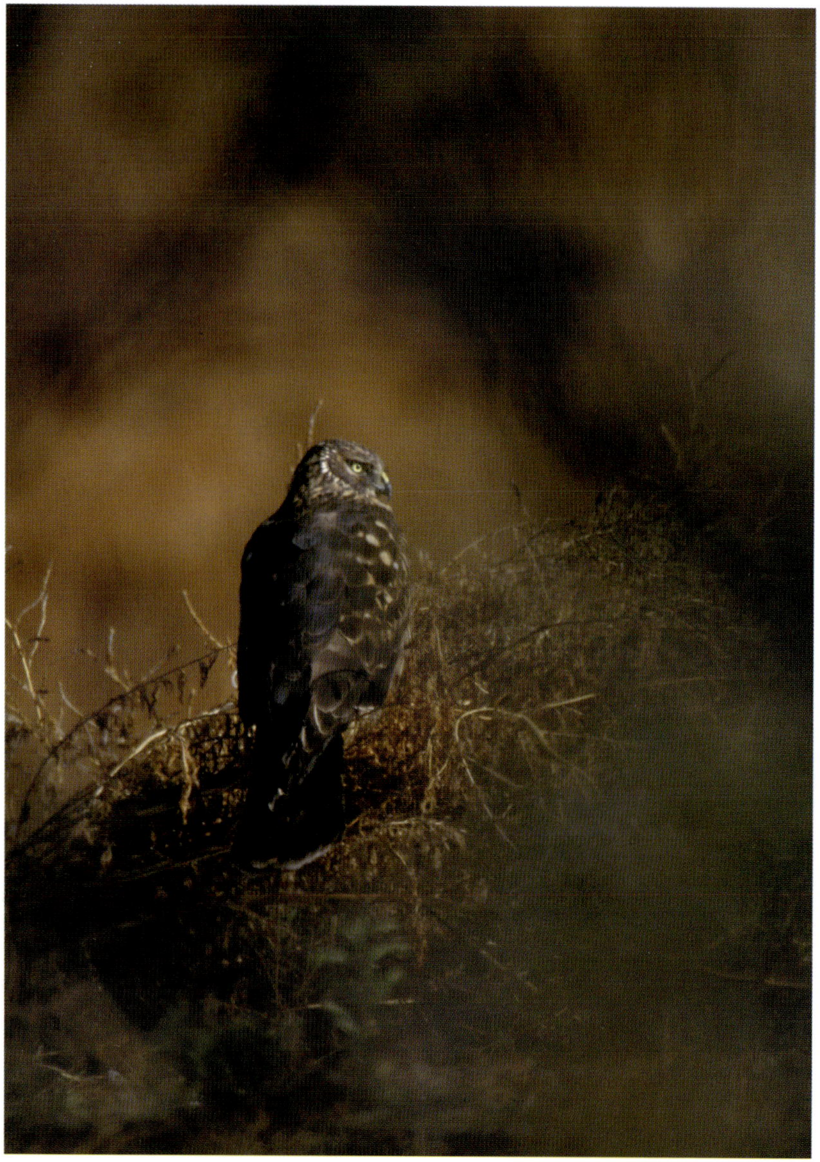

Left: Typically moving fast and low to the ground, a Northern Harrier has set down long enough to be spotted through the trees.

Right: As midday approaches, the herons return to work the small streams and irrigation channels.

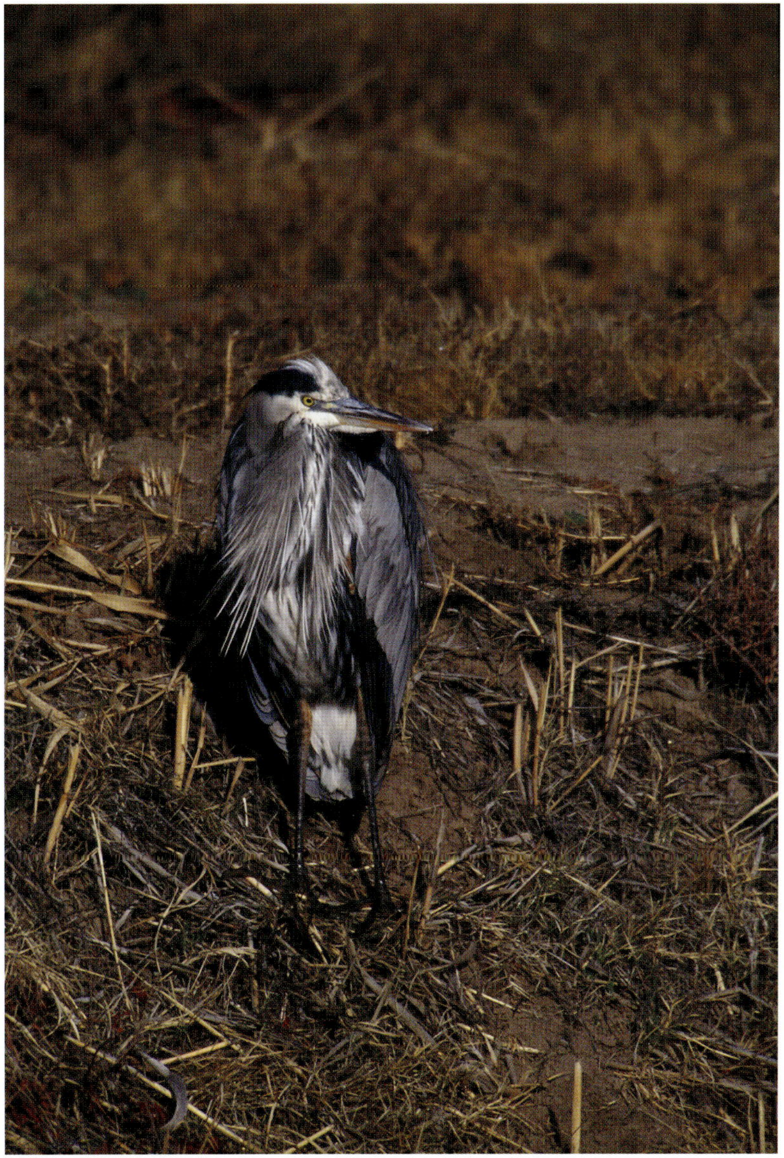

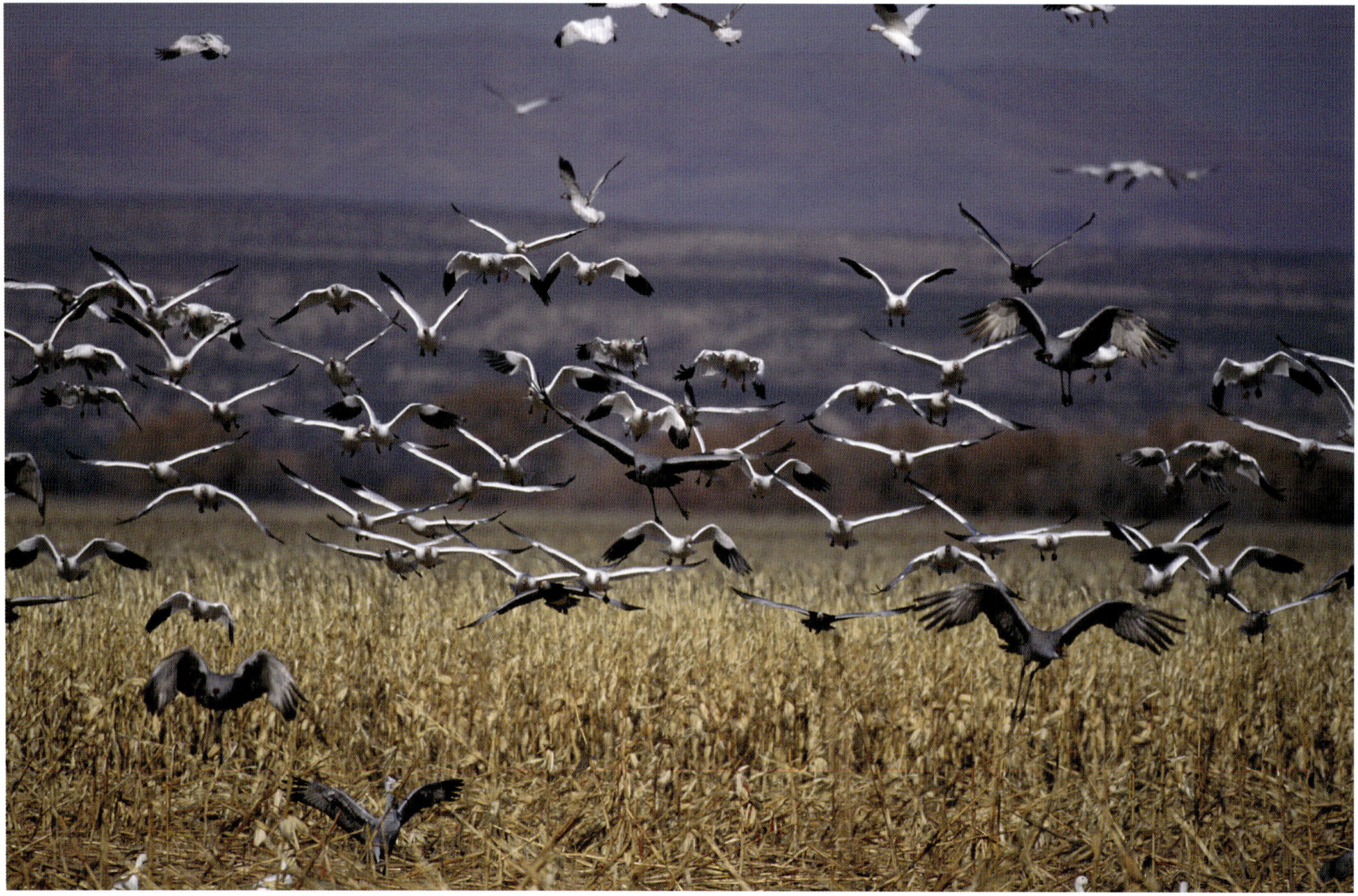

Above and Right: At the cornfield, Snow Geese and cranes continue their daily sporadic launch into flight.

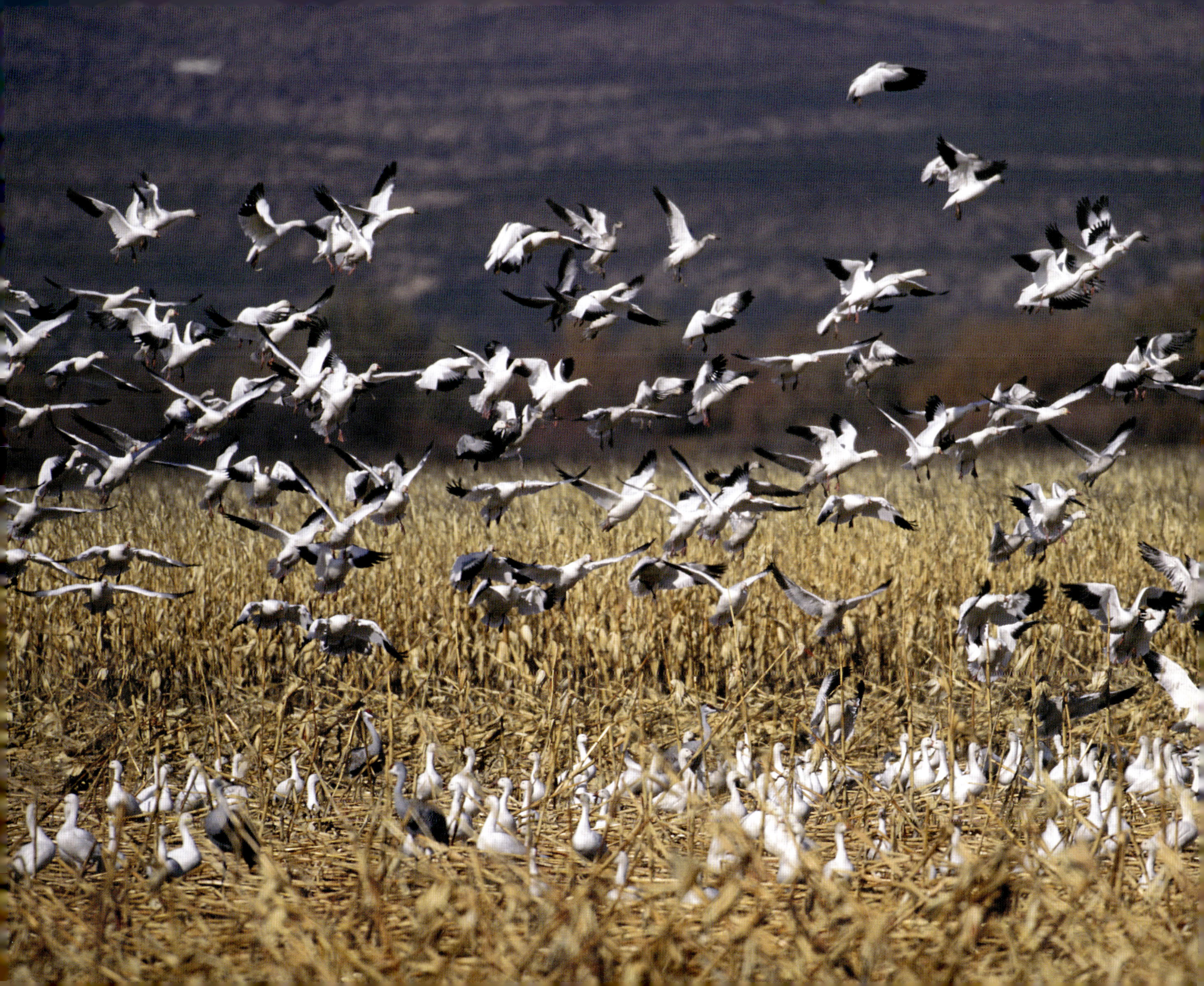

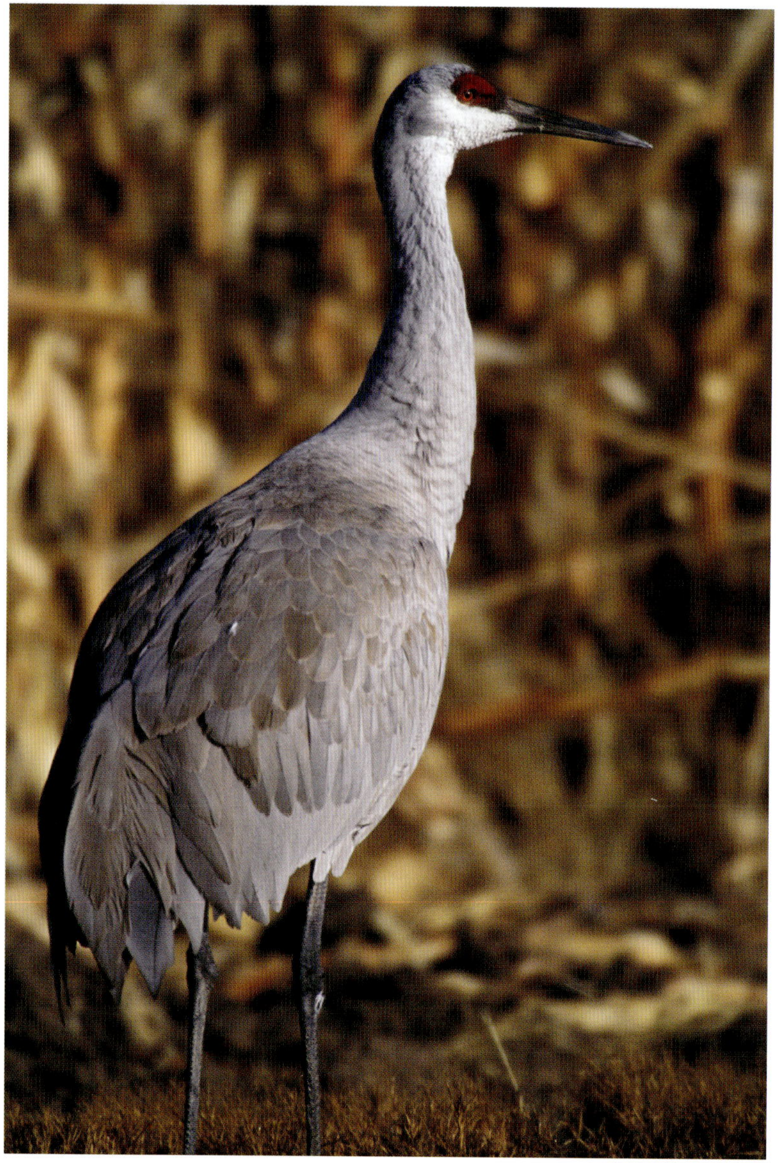

Right: Close to the auto route, cranes search for food in the adjacent cornfields.

Left: With the sun at its highest point of the day, several Sandhill Cranes call loudly to one another.

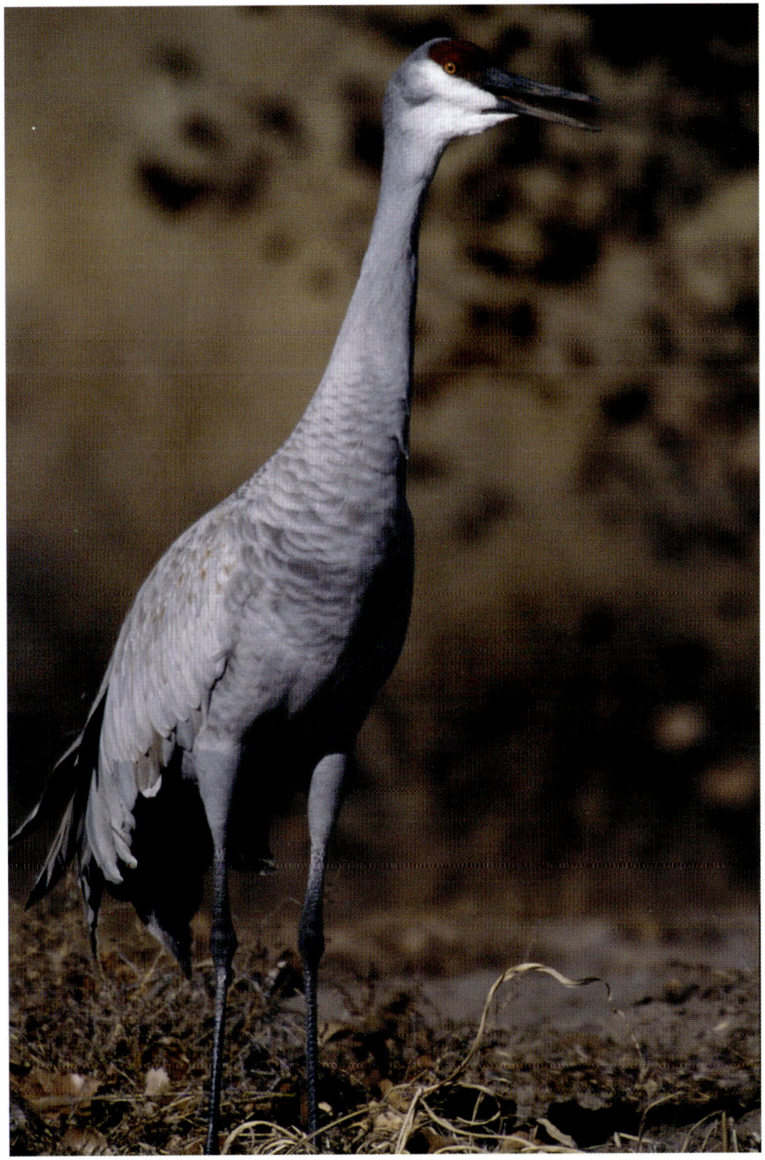

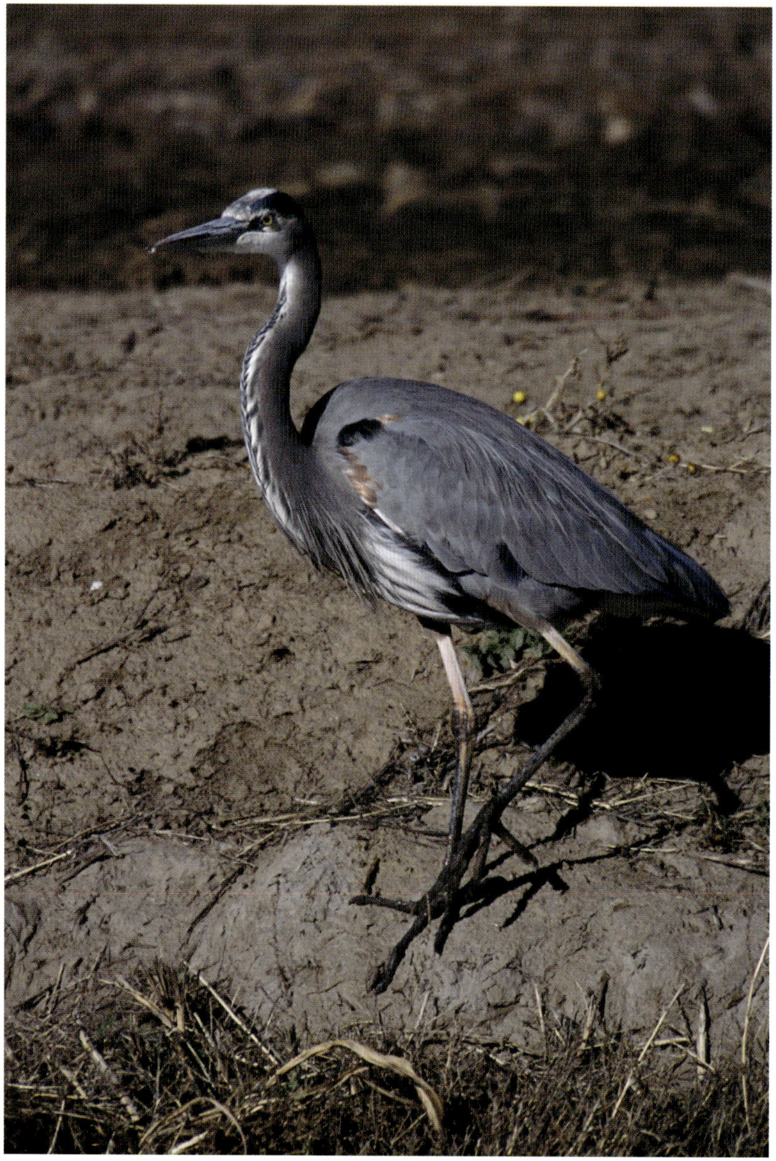

Right: Along the auto route, the same juvenile Red-tailed Hawk was discovered on the following day.

Left: This Great Blue Heron searches for fish with a careful eye to intruders.

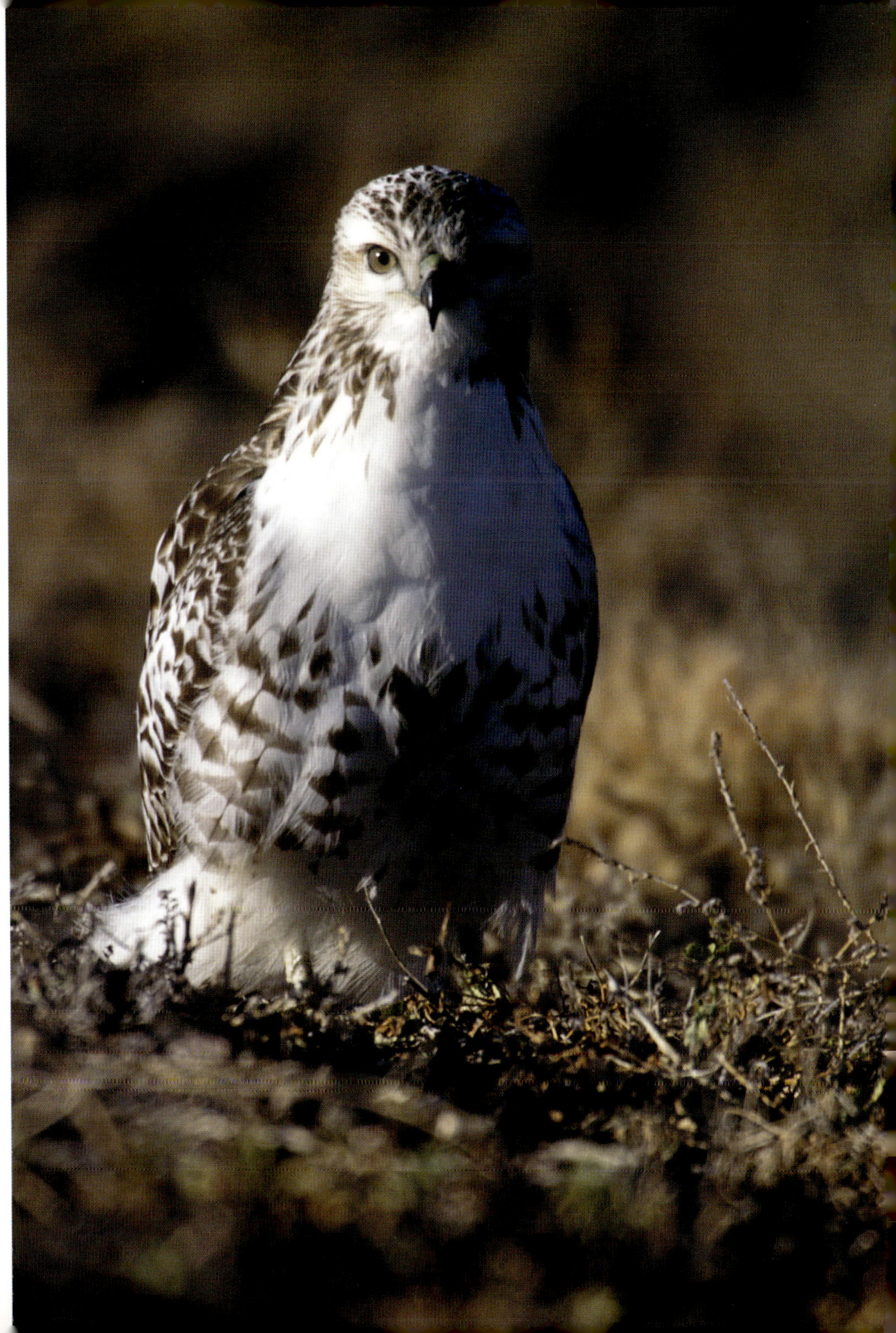

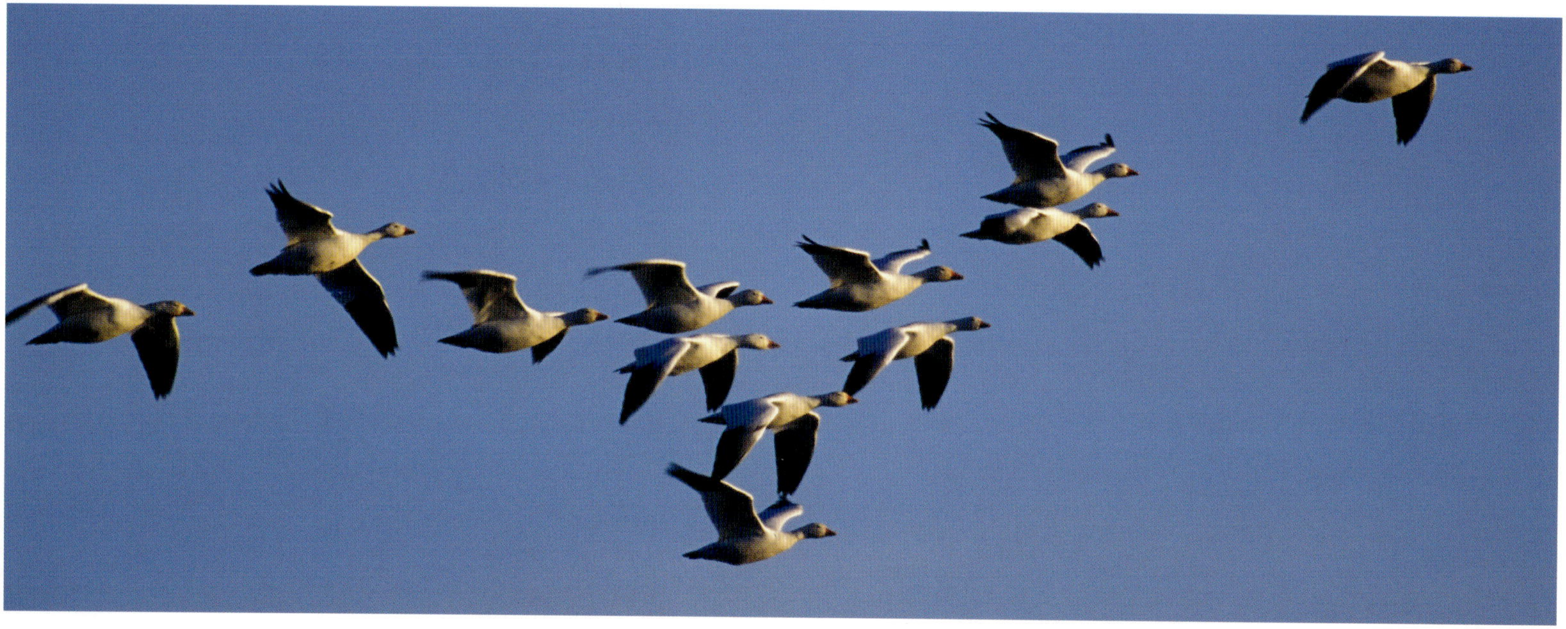

Above: With the sun quickly setting on another day, Snow Geese take to the air.

Right: As evening comes again, the New Mexico sky is full of color. High over head, the moon accentuates the clear, cold night ahead. Safety set down for the night, Sandhill Cranes assume a familiar position.

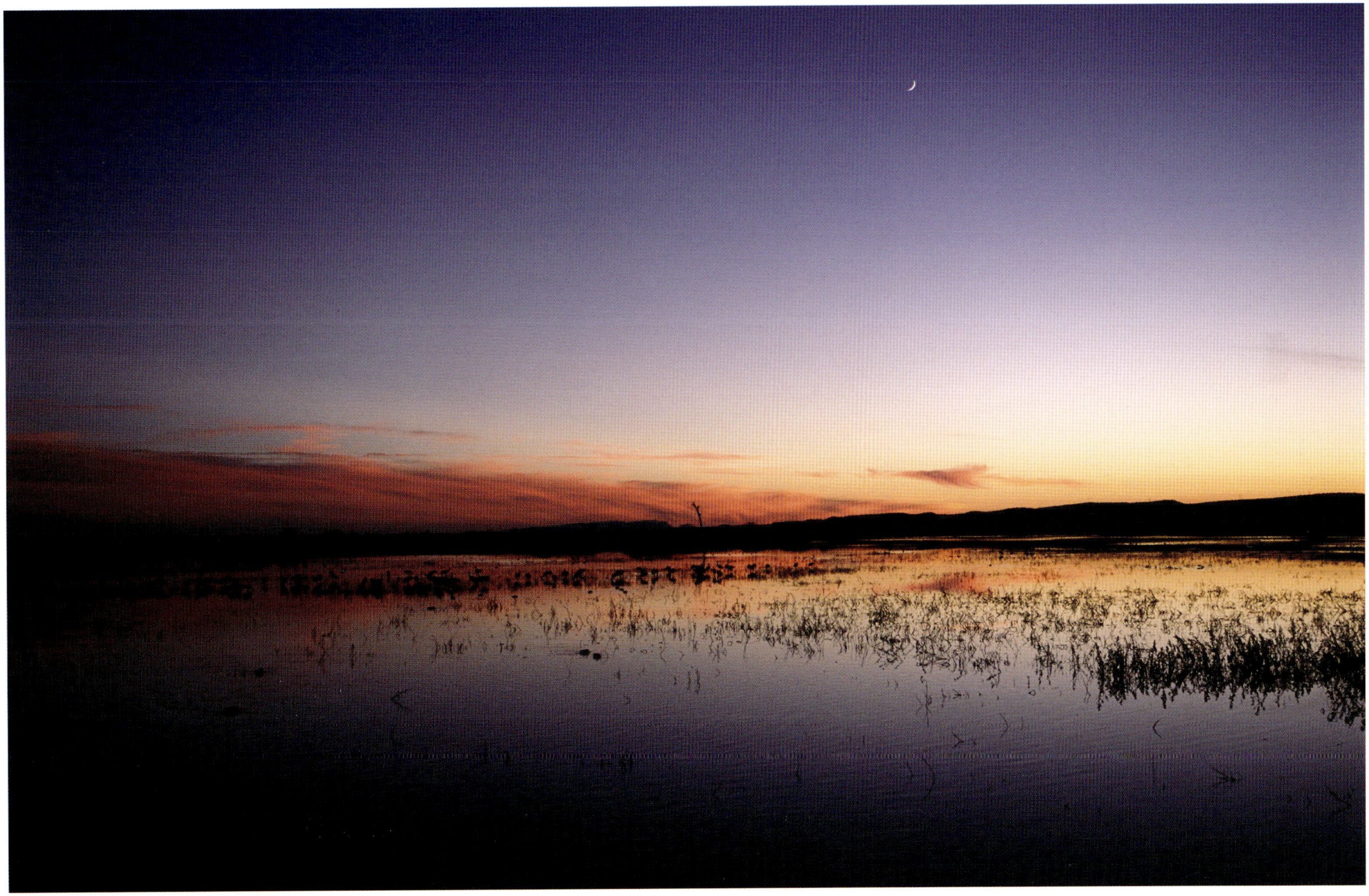

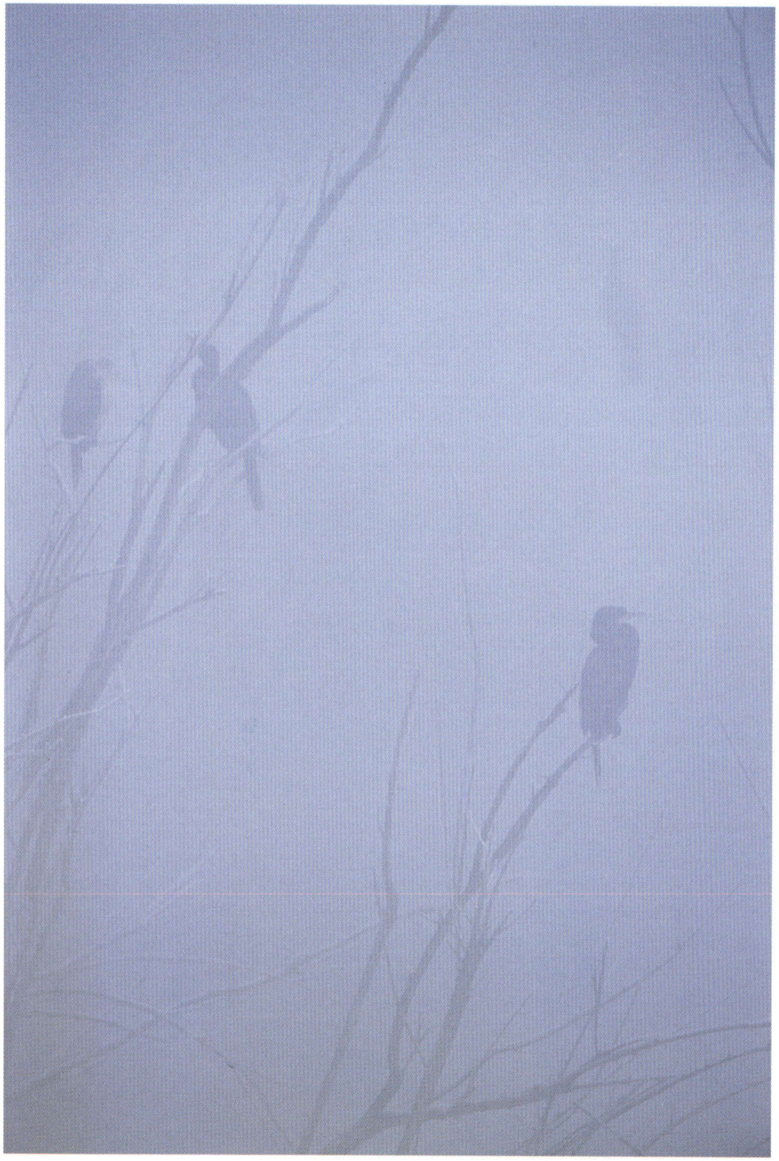

Left: As morning approached the next day, a heavy blanket of fog sits over Bosque del Apache with visibility less than 20 feet. Grounded, Cormorants roost where Snowy Egrets once maintained watch. In all directions however, massive flights of Snow Geese can be heard overhead and off in the distance. However, none can be seen.

Right: A reflecting Cormorant waits for the fog to lift and dry its wings in the warmth of the sun.

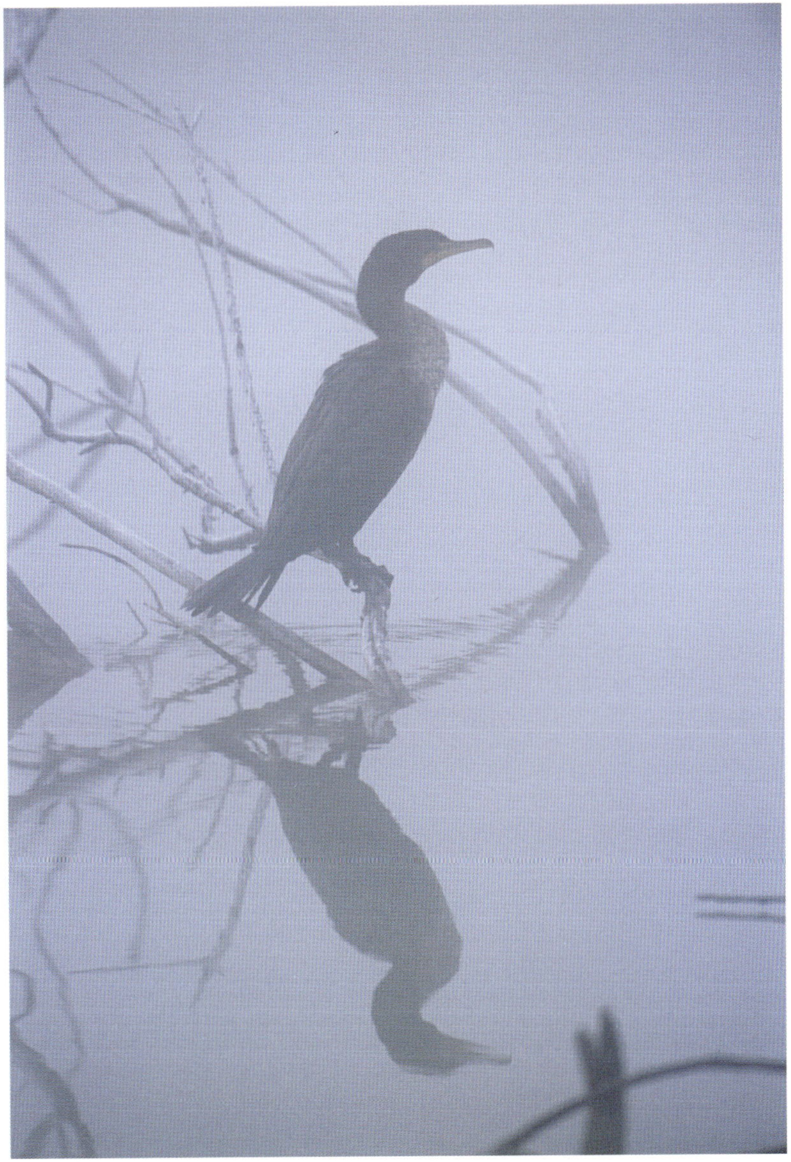

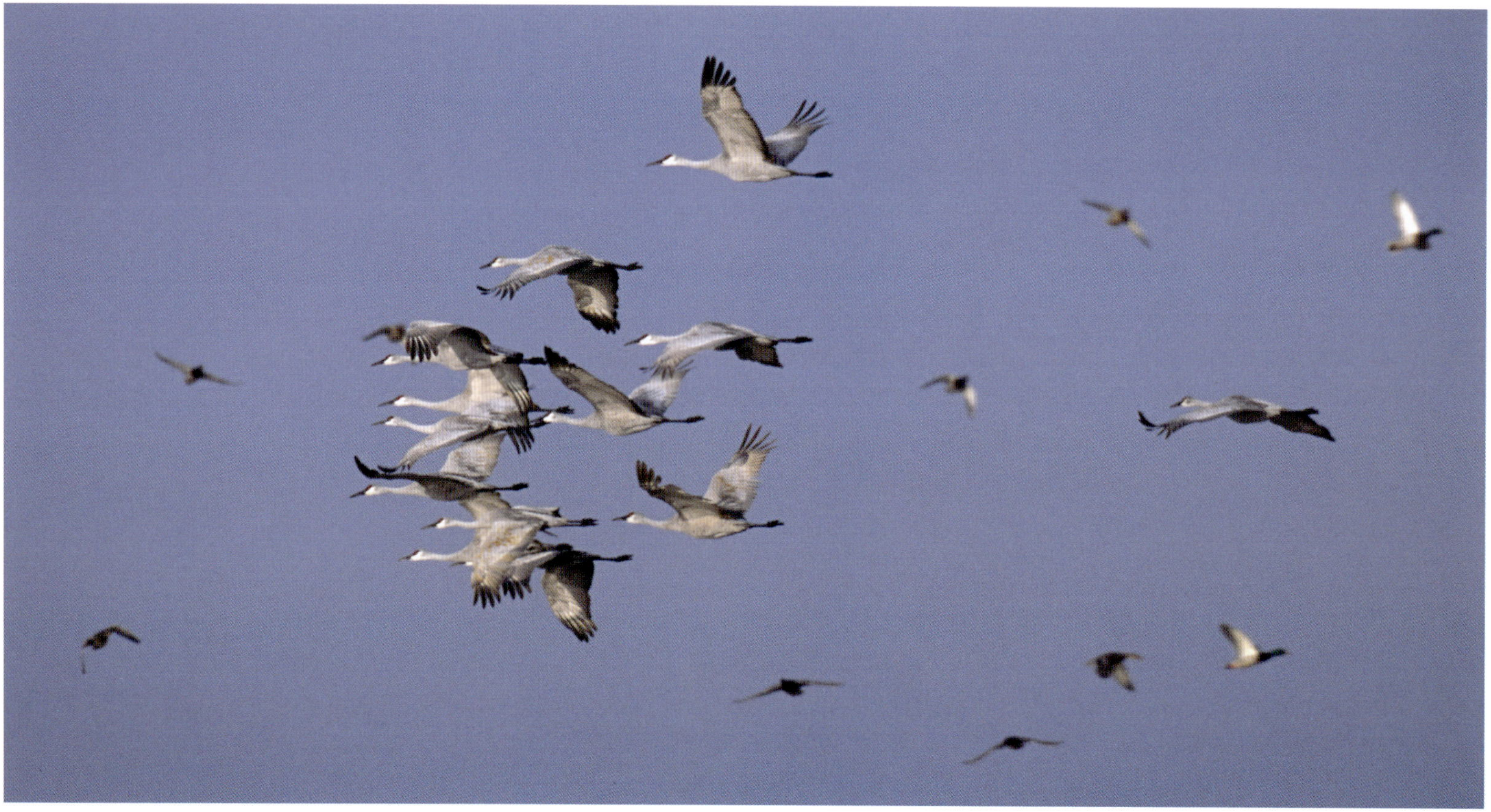

Above: As the fog burns off, Sandhill Cranes, Mallards, pintail and Snow Geese sustain the rhythm of flight and life on the refuge.

Right: Bosque del Apache hosts a large number of Mallards. Hundreds are in flight over the marsh now that the fog has lifted.

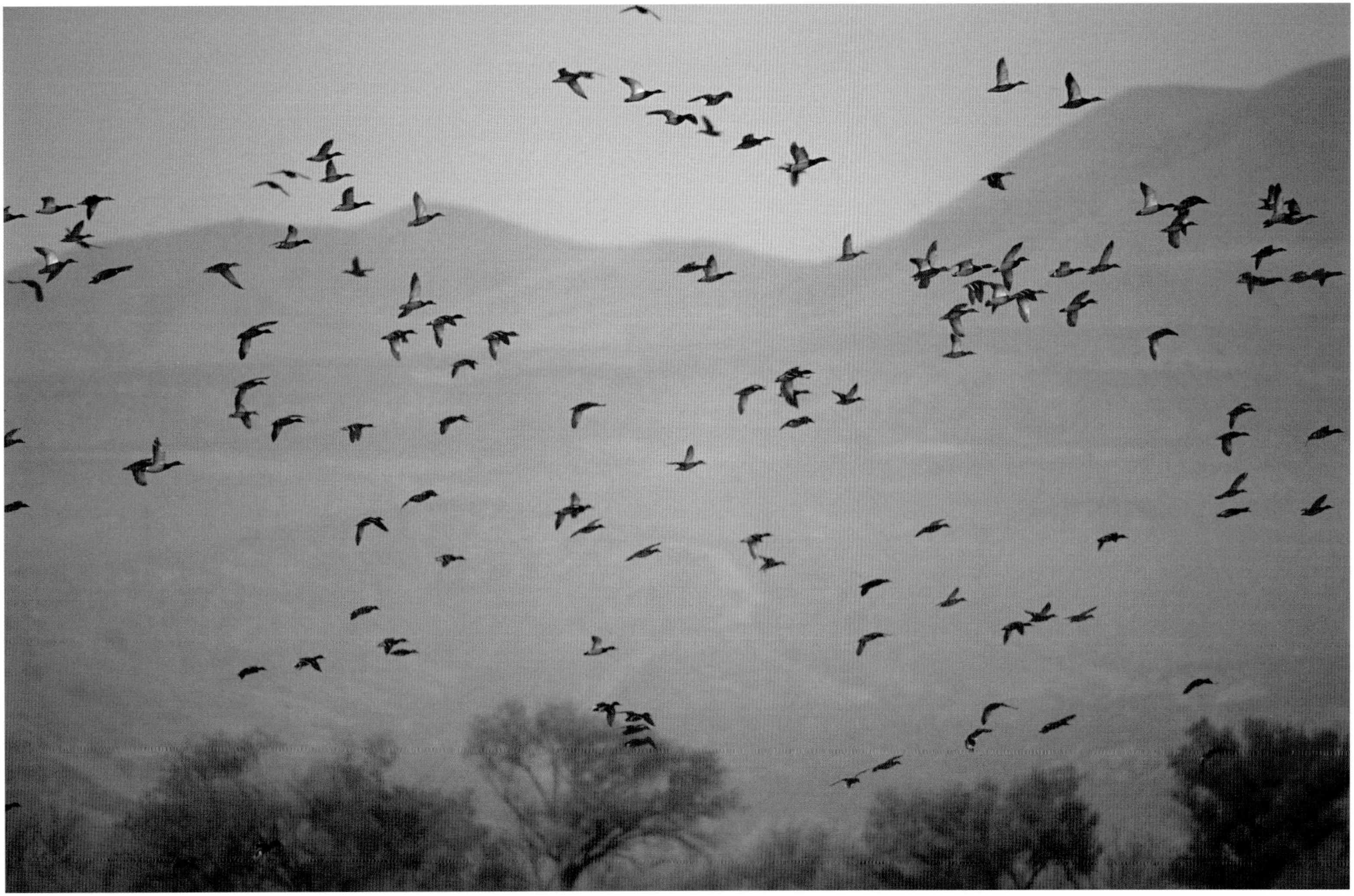

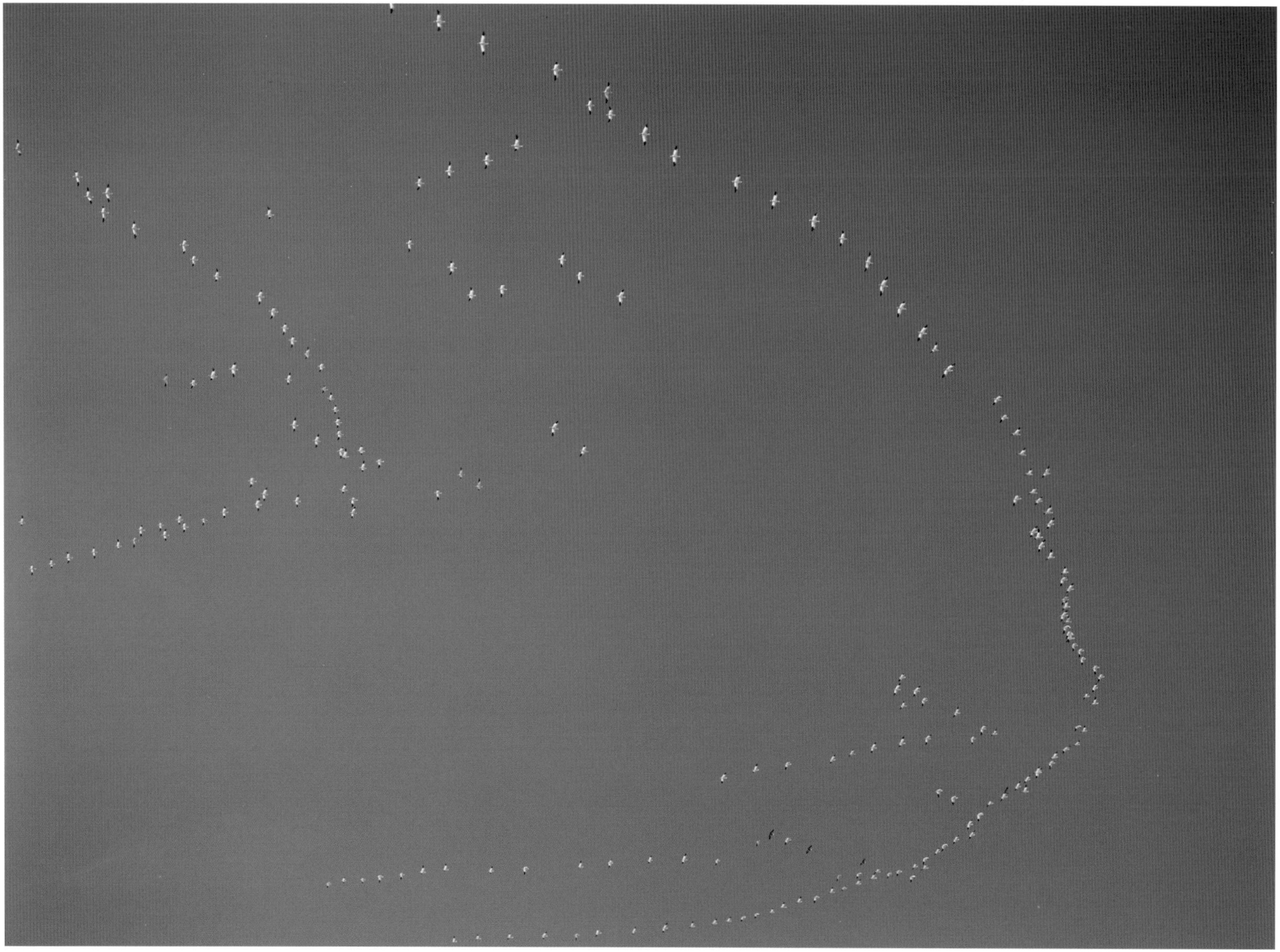

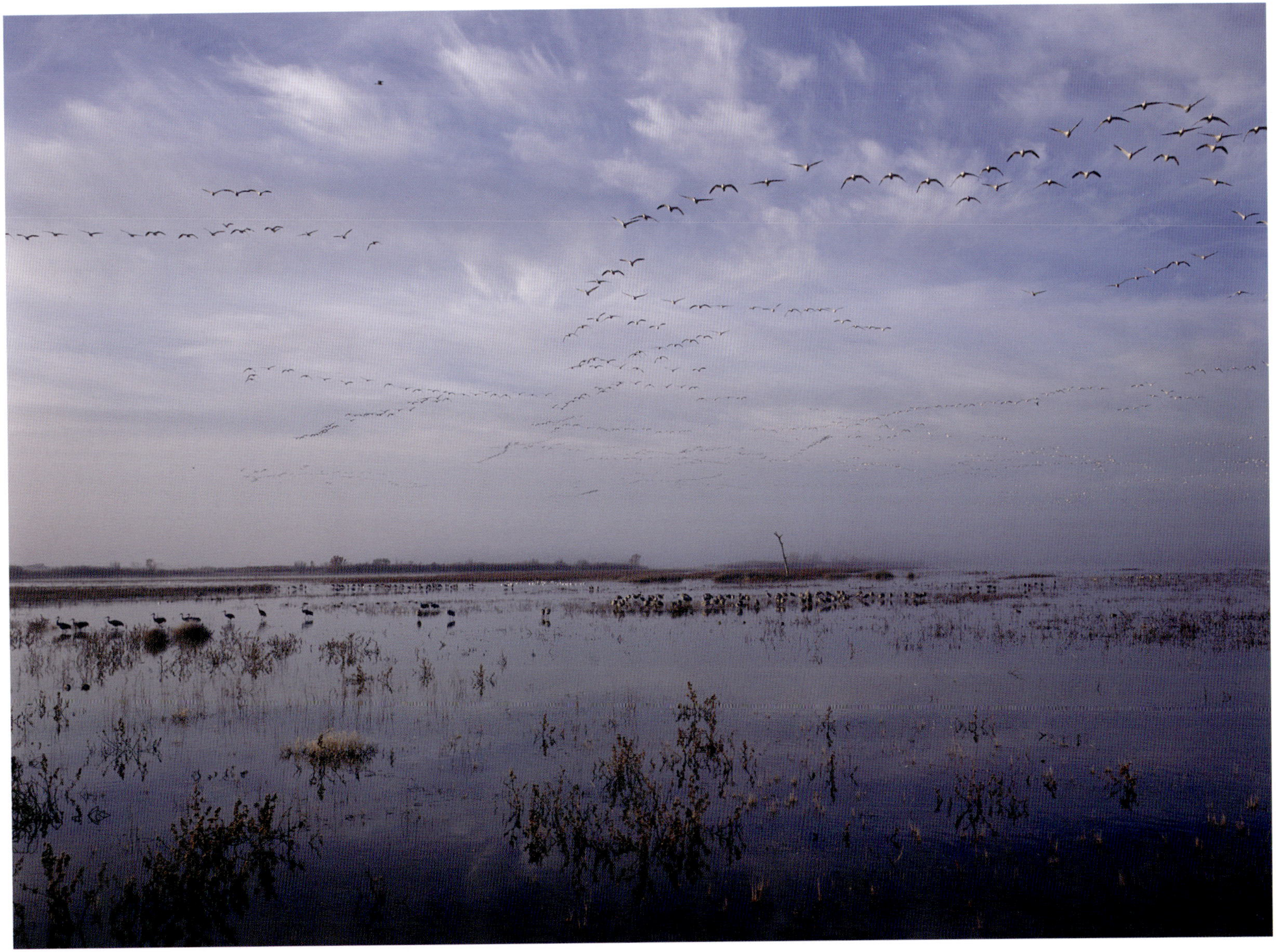

On March 14th, 1903, President Theodore Roosevelt took the first step in preserving our wildlife by establishing the Pelican Island National Wildlife Refuge in Florida. The insightful protection of this small island sanctuary not only afforded highly endangered birds the security to thrive, it set in motion conservation and preservation efforts that have continued to this very day.

Today, America's National Wildlife Refuge System comprises over 95 million acres in 540 dedicated refuges across the country. Operated by the US Fish & Wildlife Service, refuges such as Bosque del Apache provide critical protection and preservation for a wide number of species.

The influence of Bosque del Apache has been notable. In 1939, the refuge supported a handful of Sandhill Cranes and Snow Geese. Today, it hosts one of the largest concentrations of these birds worldwide and over three hundred other bird species. Wintering in a network of water and marsh areas, these birds return to the central flyways of the Midwest and Rocky Mountains each spring to be enjoyed by millions for many years to come. This could not be possible without the tireless support for preservation and sanctuary once envisioned over 100 years ago.

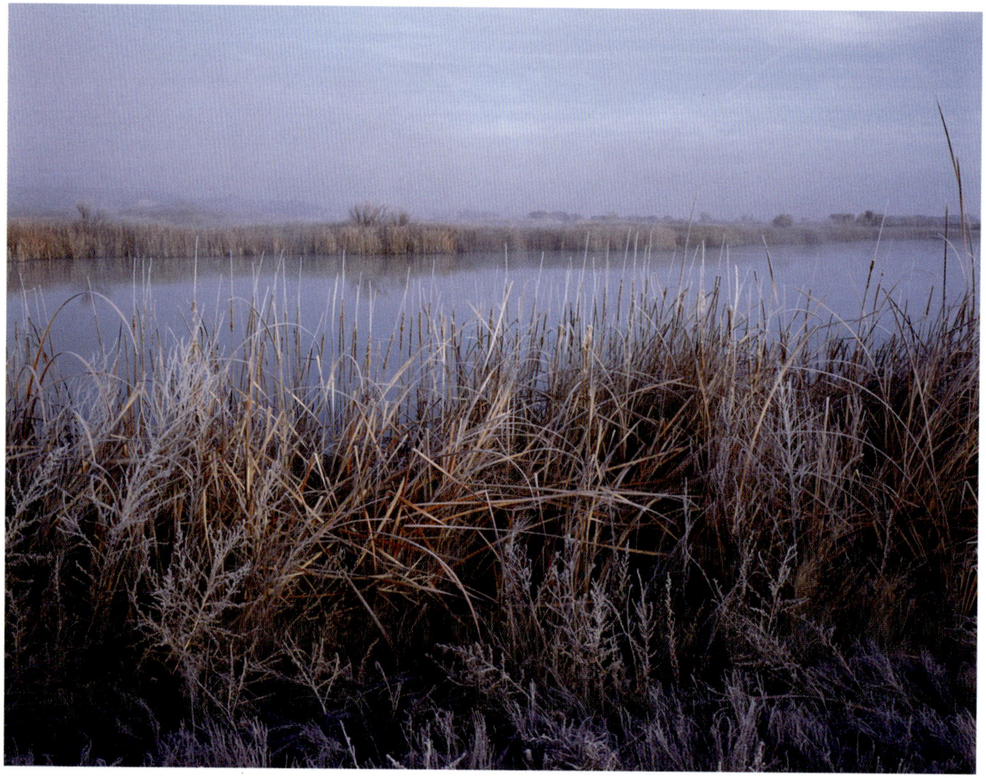

Above: Lifting fog over the expansive waterways and marsh areas of Bosque del Apache National Wildlife Refuge.